GLOWING

GLOWING

Like Fine gold

Esther Nurse

Copyright © 2022 by Esther Nurse.

Library of Congress Control Number: 2022907518
ISBN: Hardcover 978-1-6698-1925-7
Softcover 978-1-6698-1924-0
eBook 978-1-6698-1923-3

All rights reserved. No part of this book may be reproduced or transmitted in any form or by any means, electronic or mechanical, including photocopying, recording, or by any information storage and retrieval system, without permission in writing from the copyright owner.

Scripture quotations marked KJV are from the Holy Bible, King James Version (Authorized Version). First published in 1611. Quoted from the KJV Classic Reference Bible, Copyright © 1983 by The Zondervan Corporation.

Scripture quotations marked "NKJV" are taken from the New King James Version. Copyright © 1982 by Thomas Nelson, Inc. Used by permission. All rights reserved.

Scripture quotations marked (NIV) are taken from the Holy Bible, New International Version®, NIV®.

Copyright © 1973, 1978, 1984 by Biblica, Inc.™
Used by permission of Zondervan. All rights reserved worldwide.

Any people depicted in stock imagery provided by Getty Images are models, and such images are being used for illustrative purposes only.
Certain stock imagery © Getty Images.

Print information available on the last page.

Rev. date: 04/19/2022

To order additional copies of this book, contact:
Xlibris
844-714-8691
www.Xlibris.com
Orders@Xlibris.com
841818

CONTENTS

Dedication vii
Acknowledgments ix
Foreword xi
    My Self xiv

Chapter 1: The Season Of Change 1
    Embrace Me, Lord 17

Chapter 2: I Know Who Holds My Hand 19
    When The Spirit Speaks 26

Chapter 3: Finding Peace Within The Storm 28
    The Fight For My Life 33

Chapter 4: The Season Of New Challenges 36
    Charity 49
    A Beautiful Soul 51

Chapter 5: The Season Of Acceptance And Restoration 52
    Hope 57

Chapter 6: Knowing Your Worth 59
    I Looked For Someone 66

Chapter 7: Rejected No More 68

Chapter 8: Sacred Love 80
    You Are 85
    Freedom 87

My Prayer 89
Lost Love 91
Love At First Sight 93

Afterword 95

Dedication

These pages are first dedicated to my Creator, who has allowed the Holy Spirit to inspire with words that will bring joy and spiritual upliftment to every reader, including my family.

To my Grandmother, who did not live to see the legacy inscribed within her first grandchild: she who did not read or write nevertheless had a rich legacy of her own. She did her best to pass on a richness and a zeal for life. Thank you, Grandmother, for making me special in your eyes.

To my Mother, a teenager who made the choice to give me life. You were a brilliant woman who loved your children.

To my three Children, Anderson, Ibrahim, and Jadesola: As long as you allow the leading of God your Creator, He will never leave you. I am so proud of all of your accomplishments.

To my four Grandchildren, Dash, Myles, Adeyemi, Ishola: You four are bone of my bone and flesh of my flesh. May God richly bless your future as you all navigate this uncertain world.

To my New York City New Life Church Family, heartfelt thank you for holding my hands up in prayer. Words cannot express my gratitude. You are a family everyone needs to have. So many of you have encouraged me to write my story. Many thanks to the entire congregation and to all of the Pastors who have sought to motivate me for better. Pastor Oriel Thomas, Pastor Reginal Chery, and Pastor Lincoln Smith, thank you for your leadership.

Finally, to all the women and young ladies who have looked up to me for leadership, and to those women who have a story to tell but cannot tell anyone: Thank you for allowing me, through my story, to motivate you and to impress upon you to allow the Holy Spirit's transformation of your lives.

Acknowledgments

A very special thank you to my friend Rose Roxton, who motivated and kept me uplifted during my time of illness. Though you were also sick, you never left me alone. You are a special woman with a heart of gold. Glow on, my sister.

Thanks to Mrs. Sheila Hunt, who encouraged me years ago to find my own project, to focus my mind on other things in life.

My former first lady, Myrna Thomas, for your inspiration in your selection of books for my reading pleasure when times were tough for me.

My dear friend, Heather Critchlow-Baako, a kind heart who is always thinking of me. You give the best advice. Your generosity speaks volumes about your character. Continue to live your life to its fullest. Our Creator has a very special gift for you.

My son, Anderson Smith, a brilliant mind who has also been my encourager—studious, driven, and focused. Thank you, Dr. Smith.

Dr. Cicely Daly, thank you for your encouragement to push through and just write.

My Mount Calvary Church family: A heartfelt thank you is not enough. I thank everyone for their continued prayers, my anointing, and their encouragement. I am and have been blessed.

Foreword

This book is my testimony of how God has kept me, God's demonstration of love and commitment to me. I take my inspiration from the many books of the bible and poetic works.

The title of my book was inspired by a verse in the book of Exodus: Exodus 34:29, "When Moses came down from Mount Sinai with the two tables of the Covenant laws in his hand, he was not aware that his face was radiant because he had spoken with the Lord" (NIV).

Moses glowed because the glory of the Lord was upon him. His face reflected God's divine glory. God was always with Moses; however, before he could experience the glory of the glow, Moses encountered and endured some difficult situations in his life. God always had and has a plan, not only for Moses's life but for mine and yours.

I chose to use the title *Glowing* because it reflects the testimony of the many hardships I have encountered and the many seasons during my wilderness experiences. Darkness would have engulfed me, but today I am glowing because great is His faithfulness unto me.

Moses almost lost his life as a baby because of a decree. He lived in a palace but was Spirit-fed in a humble hut by a Hebrew slave mother. He lost his rights to remain in the palace. He was banished to a faraway land after a murder, sent to a place where he would learn how to be a leader, and ultimately met with the "I AM" face to face.

Moses was overcome by the pressures of the multitude and, even in his humbleness, succumbed to anger. This is just a short synopsis of the conflicts that Moses would endure, but after all his conflicts, he achieved an opportunity to glow in God's glory.

My inspirations for this book come from two sources. The first is a quote from an unknown author: "Sometimes good things have to end for better things to happen." The second is the bible, Ecclesiastes 3:1: "To everything there is a season and a time to every purpose under the heaven" (KJV).

The driving force behind this book is a tribute to growth, to new experiences, to generational legacy and renewed faith. This book comes from many periods of brokenness, emotional disappointments, multiple rejections, and serious illness. It also comes from a place of fond memories, healing, and deliverance.

I have finally arrived at a place where time permits me to express and celebrate my release from my wilderness place.

Like an evolving butterfly, the struggle has been real. Now, I just want to fly. However, even the butterfly has a waiting period before it takes flight. Yet with haste, it must take flight.

My story emulates a spiritual transparency for which only the Holy Spirit could have been the intercessor for my transformation. It is my hope that individuals reading this book will realize hope for their future, how the foundation of the past propels all of us to places beyond the past, to a present uncultivated future. It is my hope that readers will realize how specific choices aid in the representation of major transformation in their lives.

In addition, I hope readers will discern the need to allow the inner spirit to cultivate new growth, new paths, and new strength. It is never too late to find pleasure in the changes that life brings each person and to embrace the joys that each new season brings, regardless of the outcome.

I realized so many women have a story, but some of our stories are so painful that we live our lives waiting for a moment to exhale. This book is also written with an insight and a desire to motivate spiritual enhancement. Each chapter will identify seasons of realized hurts, pains, and deliverance. These are my testimonies of overcoming adversities, embracing the woman I have become, and living my desire to no longer remain a prisoner within or a slave to circumstances.

It is my hope that all who read this book will eventually come to comprehend their need for higher spiritual guidance and gain the power to find peace in the midst of their individual circumstances.

Readers will gain strength for their journey and seek to uncover, with the Holy Spirit's guidance, how faith and trust lead each man or woman to his or her freedom.

The freedom to step to the mountain means standing bravely and cultivating new paths, even if the mountain does not move.

I pray that as you read this book, you will climb to your high places with holy boldness, a commanding attitude, and noticeable peace. It is also my heartfelt hope that all those reading this book will be inspired to find the source of their glow.

The poems I include here exemplify the emotional changes we all may encounter at different intervals of our lives, but with prayer and surrender, we will develop a strong motivation for clearly defined changes.

There were times when I questioned how I found myself in the hard places—places where I was taken advantage of, where I knew emotional brokenness, broken family, loss of finances, loneliness, sickness, and countless other hard places. During my serious battle with illness, I finally decided to tell my story.

Life is full of changes. There is always a season of complete change for everyone. At that moment, you question: Why am I in chains? Where did these chains come from? Then there is a moment when you realize you have been delivered. The chains are gone! You realize your proverbial wings are flapping and you are no longer where you began. A new path, a new beginning, a new life, a new love. You have come out of the refiner's fire as fine gold, a fine pearl, and a glowing diamond.

I formed this book with eight chapters, because eight is the number for new beginnings. I am in my path of new beginnings. There are also a number of poetry readings for reflection.

MY SELF

Just a peep, a quick glance, hey who is that anyway?

A self I don't recognize

Standing in amazement, I ponder how do I introduce myself

Spending so much time looking out I didn't realize you have always been with me,

Something to behold, such poise, and such spellbinding beauty

Captivated, I take another look, Yes! She is no longer a little girl, but a woman now.

She thinks freely, she is beginning to enjoy life; Oh, but I can tell there is

something deeply invisible, dark yet seductive,

I am beckoned into the deep unknown, a woman I have never met

Yet she feels like a little girl still reaching to find her place in the world

She smiles, even her smiles speak to the heart but not my heart, her heart

Will she allow me to know her or will she creep back into herself?

I find myself longing to be like her

She has so much love to give, it is almost as if she is suffocating from the overload

Tell me again who is this self I have never met

Now that I have found you, I don't want to let you go

So secretive, so spiritually filled

Discovering her talents, discovering her strengths, discovering her imaginations,

Exploring her boundaries, yes, so fragile,

Be careful of her!

I sense something dangerous about her,

Tread softly...

Where love blooms and beauty thrive, deep danger lies

She is a lady, a very special lady

A self I never knew, a self, hidden from life's pain

But why did she surface now, could it be because she is a woman now?

Could it be because she wants to share her love now or could it be because she is full of love now?

Life's pains have not allowed her to show her true self

Looking at her now, she glows, she realizes she is a woman now

All these years, yes, she is a woman now.

Esther C. Nurse

Chapter 1

THE SEASON OF CHANGE

Becoming a Woman

Transparency at times has been difficult for me. As far back as I can remember, I have been thought to be a keeper of secrets and culturally not allowed to share the issues of home or issues that would be deemed unshareable. Somehow, something inside of me kept propelling me to my essence. That essence was to arrive at my place of bright illumination. I needed to glow.

These words are being penned to encourage the sharing of ancestral beginnings, a special lineage that is the binding thread that needles through all our generations. Perhaps going backwards actually helps a person to move forward.

These words are meant to incite spiritual and ancestral dialogue between mothers and daughters, fathers and sons. Where did we come from? Who am I? It is important to chronicle your life story, your adventures, your survival. Tell them about your life, include your hurts and the pains that build your inner psychological strength, tell them how you made it through and how you coped with life's drudgeries. But most of all tell them about your victories.

I want to share my story with the world. For too long, I have tucked away what is now overflowing within. I am filled with a legacy of storytelling, of a desire to unlock the rooms that kept me captive. To be unshackled from the wilderness that kept me wandering and from the fears that hindered my freedom. I want to share my experiences so that others may also come to glorify our God and Creator.

I begin with an uncommon and unexpected situation. This situation, though it may appear trivial, propelled me to finally finish what I have been Spirit-led to complete.

While tying up some loose ends in preparation to funeralize my mother, I entered a store. There were about three patrons, including myself. I heard the loud wails of a young lady as she ran frantically through the aisles of the store. I inquired of the store owner what was the problem. I was told she had lost one of her pearl earrings. This girl was combing the floors in heartbreaking tears. I was so moved by her distress that I began to assist in the search. I felt so empathic that I just wanted to find the earring for her.

This pearl was so valuable to the young lady that her heart was broken because it was now lost. I don't know the circumstances of how she came to receive the pearl, perhaps it was a gift from her grandmother or a family heirloom, who knows? I was so engrossed with the distress of the missing earring that I did not think to ask.

Then I thought: What about myself? Am I not like that pearl? I began to make the correlation between myself and how a pearl comes about. A pearl begins inside an oyster's shell, when a grain of sand invades the shell and its protective layer. The oyster tries to protect itself from irritation, so it begins to cover the intruder with layers of nacre, a mineral substance. Layer upon layer of this substance coats the sand, beginning the formation of an iridescent gem.

Cultured pearls are made in much the same way, only in these instances the farmer implants the obstacle within the shell. Some pearls, depending on where they is grown, can formulate within six years. Generally, saltwater pearls will take about five to twenty years. The longer the pearl stays in the shell, the larger and more beautiful it becomes. It appears to glow with its beauty.

I want to compare my life to an often-coveted gem. I was a gem with little introspective knowledge. In one of my treasured poetry collections, there is a special line from the poem "The Old Violin" by Myra Brooks Welch. The poem speaks of an old violin in which no one seemed interested until a tune was played. "The audience cheered, but some people cried, "We just don't understand…what changed its worth?" Swift came the reply: "The touch of the Master's Hand…"

There are many fine gems, like myself, that have not been discovered. But my Master, my Heavenly Father knows my worth. Ephesians 1:4-6: "Just as He chose us in Him before the foundation of the world, that we should be holy and without blame before Him in love…" (NKJ). God has demonstrated His claimed and committed love to his children.

I have learned that pearls do not just come about. It takes time under much discomfort and a desire for the oyster to free itself from that which invaded its shell. I have learned that there are multiple types of pearls. Some pearls are cultured, and some pearls are coveted from specific areas of the world. It is said that pearls from the Japanese Sea are the most desired.

I am so grateful for my origins, though humble. I began my journey from another part of the world. I was propelled to a place where I now have a desire to shine. I, like the pearl, have encountered various invasions under my proverbial shell.

My story begins like a pearl. I love the quote from Maya Angelou which says, "Pretty women wonder where my secret lies. Men themselves have wondered what they see in me…. I am a woman phenomenally. Phenomenal woman, that's me." I reference this poem because life has not been a breeze for me.

We women are all phenomenal in many aspects of our lives, and there are some phenomenal men, too. A Spirit-filled woman recognizes such a man. But women are especially precious. Regardless of your life's encounters, do not allow anyone to trample on your preciousness.

As far back as I can remember, my life had some interesting beginnings. As a young girl growing up in South America, I never had that coveted mother-daughter closeness that many daughters were privileged to have with their mothers. Perhaps it was because my mother was a child herself at my conception.

She was sixteen, my father seventeen. Some point between my birth and the age of six, my mother left her baby. I would be without the bonding relationship of my mother and raised by my grandmother. Something went wrong between my mother and my grandmother.

The short end of the story: I learned that my grandmother told my mother to go but to leave the baby. I do not know how my grandmother cared for me by herself. I guess that was the genesis of single parenthood in my family. I eventually became a part of the statistics.

I was six years old when my grandmother introduced me to my mother—a woman I had not known or knew about. She was a stranger to me, and hearing the words from my grandmother—"This is your mother"—had a resounding strangeness.

I recalled feeling shy at our first encounter. I had returned home after school to be introduced to a woman lying in bed at my grandmother's home. I was a little girl who did not know the woman before me. She had returned home to my grandmother's home, after six years of leaving her baby.

The woman I was being introduced to had some kind of illness. She was just lying in the bed, looking helpless. At the time, I did not comprehend what was happening. She did not say much to me, and there were no hugs, no form of touch. She did not know me either. When she spoke, the only request she had was "Show me the latest dance moves." I recalled dancing for her, then retreating to my shy place. In the days and months that followed, I learned my mother was going to have a baby.

This was something I knew nothing about. I believe I only understood what that meant when I saw the baby. The night my baby brother was born, I accompanied my grandmother in the very early hours of the morning to find the only midwife in the village. My grandmother and I walked about three to five miles to arrive at the midwife's home. Phones were not available in those days. Messages traveled via in-person appearances or word of mouth.

Little did I know that I would become the caretaker of this little boy, a new addition to the family. I was six years old when I became what people in the South call a "knee mama"—someone who cares for siblings like a mother. My job now was to know the new baby while getting to know my new mother.

I carried that boy everywhere. If I needed to carry water in a bucket, he was cradled with one hand while I carried him on one hip; the bucket and water were in my other hand. I had to learn to change his cloth diapers and feed him. I was required to do some of the washing. When my mother was not breastfeeding, it was my job to care for him. Later as the years followed, I would have to assist with five more siblings.

I began to be pushed further and further back from the embrace of the true love of a mother. I later became known as the eldest of seven, having the handed-down, expected responsibility to care for my siblings.

I am still identified by my siblings as the oldest and the Matriarch. I suppose that is fitting, as I have stashed away in my deepest memories the stories of my childhood, the nighttime songs taught to me by my grandmother, and all the family secrets.

Tell your children that some things in their life will at times mimic a parallel similitude. There will be turns in life that will be unrecognizable with many questions…and a great search for answers.

Tell your children that they will become adults who will eventually create their own paths, memories, and life lessons. But they should always reflect on their ancestral beginnings.

Tell them to stay in the will of God: "…In all their way, acknowledge Him and He will direct their path" (Proverbs 3:5-6, KJV). They are to allow God to choose their way, confirm their way, and clear their obstacles. As I complete this book, the realization of God's directions and protective love has become more prominent. I have realized that the wilderness is a painful, lonely, deserted place and a discomfort to one's soul. I have learned that God wanted me to leave the corners of my life so that He can move in the center of my life. He wants to be my everything. Isaiah 43:1 says, "But now, thus says the Lord, who created you, O Jacob, and He who formed you, O Israel: "Fear not, for I have redeemed you; I have called you by your name; you are Mine" (NKJV). God has claimed you and me. He has adopted us to His family that we might live a bountiful, holy, and loved life.

Treat and feed your children with the wisdom of the woman or man you would like to see them become, and the manhood you would like to cultivate within your sons. Fill your sons and daughter with as much as you can as early as you can.

Teach them that God's word is the food of life, that prayer is their communicating friendship with God, that it is God who gives wisdom and they should remain steadfast in the protective care of God. Teach them the way, the truth, and the life.

Many of us are sometimes under the misguided assumption that we have time—time to share all that we want, time to shape, and time to reach back. I say speak to your daughters and your sons now, speak spiritually into and over their lives.

I have been procrastinating the completion of my Will—not because I fear death but because I believe I do not have much to leave my children, beyond the counting. But I have realized, regardless of material things or the money I do not have, the best gift or treasure I could give to them is to tell them about their lineage.

I recalled a conversation I had with my daughter many years ago. She was angry that I was having problems with a love relationship; she wanted her life to be different. Her comment to me was that she would never have the problems I had because she would take a different path. I wanted to enlighten her that sometimes one needs to comprehend the history and path of one's lineage before one can have a clearer understanding of self or what one's parents might have endured.

I wanted to ask my daughter: How do you know where you are going if you don't know where you are coming from? Suffice it to say, my concerns were not as important at the time. God is now allowing my daughter to have her own relationship and her own children. Life has a strange way of coming full circle.

In the year 2017-2018, I became ill with stomach Stage I cancer. My mother was also lying in her sick bed. As I watched my mother lying in what would become her deathbed, I had so many questions. I was in a race to learn and retain all that I could glean from her.

I just wanted her to talk. I had so many questions. It was difficult to get her to really talk to me as I needed. She was sick and looming on deep depression. She was never a talkative woman to begin with. She spent many of her last days only answering my questions with a yes or no. At times, she had no response, only a smile.

I was a woman with empty holes of my mother's love for me. During this time of her illness, I just wanted her to love me. I wanted her to tell me: Why was I so different? Why did she leave me? How come she never took the time to teach me what I needed to be a strong woman? The questions were insurmountable. My mother would leave me, and I would be left incomplete.

I reflected on the day my life as a nine-year-old girl would change forever—even then, there was no motherly advice. I would cross the threshold of womanhood, reading a book, *On Becoming a Woman*. I did not understand it, but I was told I would understand. This was typical of Caribbean/South American mothers and grandmothers.

My mother eventually sold my book to a neighbor's daughter. I was so hurt because that was my book. Everything inside was personal to only me. The book was my only teacher.

In my home, what a child discovered was only learned in spoken parables or it was read. Such was my household. A young girl learned quickly to interpret the recited daily parables which were used as a teaching tool. I knew no other way.

Prior to my mother's illness, she was a vibrant woman, with a zeal for knowledge. She was a brilliant woman with a determination to accomplish her goals. She was a poet who wrote the most beautiful and creative poems. She became a college graduate, accomplishing her dream degree—not one but two degrees—at the age of sixty-three.

My mother suffered from diabetes for more than thirty years. The beginning of her demise was the loss of her sight in one eye, then the loss of one leg, then a major heart attack, multiple surgeries, and life support twice. She finally succumbed to the icy cold hands of death one Friday morning in December of 2018. Her heart just stopped. She was gone.

Many questions were left unanswered. My life is still lacking and unsettled. So much she had not seen; I wanted her at my always projected wedding. There was so much I wanted her to be a part of. The time was too short, and I felt cheated and alone.

In my reminiscing, one day I was able to ask her a question, but I was not certain I would receive an answer. "Mommy," I said, "How do you cope with just lying in this bed?" She looked at me and said, "You just have to cope." Sounded like an answer without an answer, but as I pondered the abstractness of her response, I could only conclude it is the same response I would have given my daughter.

I have realized that not everything can be explained in extensive detail, especially when the only option my mother had was to be cared for by strangers. Her life now was dependent on the daily ingestion of pills and the anticipated wait for a loving family face to visit with her. My mother was lying in a cold, impersonal nursing home room. This would be her home for about eighteen months.

Sometimes, we could have avoided several collision courses in our lives if we had only listened. I have been on many such courses, not because of not listening but because of lack of directives.

I was often left alone as a young girl. I learned to become a loner and, at the same time, a leader. Many of my experiences could have had better outcomes, perhaps, but instead, from as early as five years of age, I had to learn to develop the strength of independence.

I recall during one of those alone days, while I walked alone on what could be deemed a two-mile journey, I was on my way to meet with my grandmother. I was about five years old then. I was chased and bitten by a dog.

I remember being taken to the hospital and again left in a room alone while I waited for treatment. In my earliest experiences, I learned how to cope with aloneness. I learned to play alone, I walked to school alone, I returned home alone, at times not certain when someone would arrive home. Sometimes there was insufficient oil to light the lamps, so I sat in the dark alone, waiting for my grandmother to return home.

As I reflect on my childhood, I realize every step of the way, God has been with me. Angels were always watching over me. Therefore, I was never really alone. As I write these words, I am in amazement at the protection of a God who knew me before I was formed in my mother's belly. Great is His faithfulness.

Help the young woman or young man in your life to understand clearly who she or he is and what genealogy flows within their veins. Sometimes our children do not have an idea of the strength of a mother, the paths and sacrifices that has allowed her to grow, and even the choices she took to ensure that her children would also become survivors.

I cannot continue without a depiction of my grandmother. She is the only and original link to the family lineage. Born in November, 1914, under British rule, she became a mother to me.

I was not allowed to have my parents' last name as they were both teenagers when I was born. Under British rule and laws, the child only received the last name of the person married in the family. So, my grandmother became my caretaker and I was known by her last name.

My grandmother was born the only child for her mother, my mother was the only child for her, and for six years, I was the only child for my mother. When my mother went to explore the world, I was left to be raised by my grandmother who did her best to care for me.

At times, I did not comprehend her moods, her methods, and her reactions towards me. Although she never spoke directly, she seemed to have some resentment towards my mother for having a child and leaving me alone. My grandmother would often laugh and talk to herself while she weeded or tended her yard. She enjoyed reaping from her prized avocado trees.

My grandmother was a storyteller. She could tell a story that would stir and spellbind the imagination of any child. Of course, these stories were only told as she was moved between moods and, at times, what seemed to be atmospheric changes to a little girl.

She had an uncanny connection to nature. I learned to read time from the position of the sun. She was always right when the sun was in a particular position. I could hear her say, "It's twelve o'clock. See how the sun stands up like a man." This meant at this hour, the sun was at its hottest, and it appeared to be positioned directly in the center of the sky. She knew when it was approaching specific hours in the day, especially at sundown; the crickets would begin to make their sounds.

She knew all the cycles of the moon. It was said I was born during a full moon because my face was so round. I don't know what a half-moon baby face looks like, but that is another story. All this from a woman who did not read or write.

It seemed that my grandmother's stories always had a never-ending continuation with a twist that created closeness, bonding you with your ancestry. During some of her revelations, there were times she reflected on her own upbringing. She talked about not being allowed to attend school because she was told girls did not attend school. They would get husbands to care for them.

As a young child, I was told stories of the little she remembered about her mother. My lineage seems to end with the slim pickings of memory of my great-grandmother.

My grandmother did not seem to have a lot of memory of a relationship with her mother because, during her young years, she was sent to live with her aunts. She called them her great-aunts. Yet my grandmother longed for a loving relationship with her mother. She told me stories of walking for miles to dress and comb her mother's hair when she heard that her mother had passed away. The care of her mother's dead body was the final attempt to receive the love she had always longed for as a girl. How interesting, these generational passages.

My grandmother told stories of abuse and starvation by her aunts. She told stories of fights she got into as a young woman. She talked about only being allowed to cook, wash, iron, and clean people's houses; she was not afforded the opportunity of receiving an education. So, these daunting chores became her trade. What she longed for was to read and write.

My grandmother told stories that helped to shape my character, leaving me with a longing to become half the woman she was. She was a woman of strength and a woman with a toughness that one could have sometimes interpreted as a lack of care and love. She was sometimes cold and argumentative without a reason for the origin of the change in attitude or mood.

She spent long hours alone. She had possibly one or two persons she spoke with or called friends. She trusted no one. She was a woman who spent much of her time alone and frowned upon the invitation of groups of people at her home or in her yard. So, I was never encouraged to have many friends. You guessed it. I have very few friends and am only close to one or two

My grandmother believed she was from a tribe in Africa who spoke Swahili. She had lost connection with her ancestry and could only recall a few words from this language. She did not know the original country. There are only a few countries in Africa that still speak Swahili.

When my grandmother became angry, I swore she was from the Zulu tribe of South Africa. She could wield her cutlass (machete) like a fierce warrior and lacked no hesitation to use it, if threatened. She was a fighter for her rights. She lacked book knowledge, yet she was the smartest person I knew. She left me with a longing to not only travel to Africa but to find out who I really am.

Born in Guyana, South America, my grandmother was an attractive Guyanese woman, slender with a dark complexion. She had long black natural hair which she braided, pinned together to conceal its length. There was some superstition that people should not know the length of one's hair. Her eyes were a dark shade of gray. When I looked at her, she was simply beautiful.

I don't recall my grandmother ever hugging me, but then that was not our cultural way. She loved me, but outward public affections were not her way. I was always well fed and clothed. She believed in feeding me. When she had money or was in the best of moods, I was often treated to my favorite chocolate milk and whatever food I wanted to eat. I was fatter than the other children in the village, so I was nicknamed "Fatty." Though never hugged me, her love for me was deeply implied. It was underlined, it was somehow taboo to even have any emotions or show of affection.

Strange, but I love affection. I look to receive and give affection, especially whenever I discern it is needed or arbitrary. I am glad I did not inherit the trait of lack of affection.

My grandmother enjoyed singing. When she was in the mood, she sang me to sleep with her old songs. Somehow, I got the feeling she felt some distress for me, and the best way to express her distress was to sing. She had a crooning type of voice, like Nat King Cole, and she loved to dance. She found a reason to dance, even if it was by herself. The night before she passed away, she was remembered as having a "good dance" show for the neighbors. She was eighty-nine years old and full of life. She was truly a blessed woman; she never lost any of her faculties and was never bedridden. My grandmother was a stubborn old woman who knew what she wanted and did it her way.

Moonlit nights in our small village were the best time for storytelling. These were the nights when the family would gather on the outside steps of the house. Most South American homes were built on stilts with outside steps that led to the entrance of the home.

Everyone would be treated to an epilogue of family history and strange stories of bats turning into humans and snakes swallowing humans whole, and of her childhood growing under the care of her aunts. She talked of instances of abuse and hard times in her life.

My grandmother enjoyed telling riddles that were difficult to figure out. This woman with limited book knowledge was full of wisdom. Little did I know I was a scribe in training. I was special in her eyes. She called me her "little company."

My grandmother was a mild-mannered woman at times. She never cried—at least I was never privy to that emotion. She worked hard for a living. She would wash other people's clothing, clean their houses, and when she was not doing those activities, she was buying and selling produce. She had nothing more than a third-grade education, but her sarcastic vocabulary was comparable to the satire of the best poets. She had a beautiful heart, and I think I inherited it. She was my phenomenal woman.

I know that I am like her because after her passing, people were astonished by recognizing her character in me. My grandmother woke up early to go on walks by herself or to begin her day's chores. The villagers were spooked the morning before her burial, when they observed me walking the same path my grandmother took on her early morning walks.

My grandmother was always in conversation with herself (which she seemed to enjoy exclusively). Sometimes I would hear her laughing heartily, even though there was no one to share the laughter with her. She found her joy within. She faced all of her disappointments and died just as she lived, quietly. She was a beautiful soul. I am proud to have been born in her genealogy.

I grew up in a humble home. It was a tiny wood house covered by zinc. The house had two bedrooms. The larger of the bedrooms was separated by a curtain to give a demarcation of the living room space and the bedroom. The other bedroom was off from the tiny kitchen. There was one window in the bedroom, one in the living room (which was also the dining room), one in the kitchen, and two in the small bedroom off from the kitchen. The entrance to the home had a two-part door; the top half could be opened while the bottom half was closed. We locked our doors with a padlock. The wooden windows had bolts. The house could be compared to an old slave shack. It was a tiny house, but it was cozy. It was the home built by my grandmother's husband. The house is no longer there. The wood that was not destroyed by the elements, but were stolen by, I want to say, those in need.

We cooked on a coal pot, although there were rare occasions when we were privy to a one-burner kerosene oil stove. We washed dishes on a stool-like table that was outside in the yard. We ate at a small dining table. We washed clothes in a container with a scrubbing board. There were times we went to wash at the creek. Clothes were hung to dry on an outside line with wooden clothespins.

We ironed with a type of cast-iron device that sometimes had a wooden handle or cloth was wrapped around a metal handle to reduce the heat. The iron was heated over the coal pot. Clothing was often starched. My grandmother believed in clothes looking well presented. My school skirts were always neatly pressed, every pleat in its place. Sometimes the pleats were so well done, I did not want to disturb the neatness by sitting on them.

When we did not collect rainwater in the two drums or barrels we had, we fetched water from a creek or from government-installed pipes. We carried water in a container on our heads or in buckets to fill our drums or barrels. The water was used for cooking, washing our feet before entering the home, washing clothes, and bathing.

We had a latrine (outhouse) or toilet in the back of the yard. When not able to use the latrine at night, we used a potty (it looked like a large teacup). Children had tiny potties until they graduated to large ones like their parents. Of course, we learned this custom from the British.

My grandmother was always saving some money; she was a "safety pin" (one who saves money). She always had money somewhere in the house for a rainy day (unexpected expenses). She would hide money under the linoleum or in a handkerchief that she carried in her bosom or pinned to her petticoat (slip). She said, "Hide your money in plain sight." According to her, anyone with intent to steal would not look for the obvious. According to my grandmother, they would be walking on her money and not even know it. When she passed away, true to her name, the family found money everywhere; she even left her tithes in an envelope. To God be the glory. As for me, well....

I always slept in my grandmother's bed; her bed never had a mattress. She had some flat wooden boards that she placed across the bed frame. She would spread old clothes to cover the bed. This bedding would be the mattress. She made patchwork sheets from old scraps of cloth. To this day, I am a lover of patchwork quilts. I think they are simply exotic and beautiful.

The yard was always swept clean with a broom made from bony coconut tree branches. Our yard was filled with various fruit trees. At the front of the house was a large guava tree; this tree was my hiding place when I did not want to be found by my grandmother. I would sometimes climb, sit in the tree, and watch her as she looked everywhere for me.

Surrounding the house were several varieties of avocado pear trees. We had several other fruit-bearing trees, including two coconut trees. We had a large yard that was fenced. Lining the front of the yard were several white lily and red hibiscus plants. There was also a cashew fat-pork (a type of fruit) tree.

I recall having two parakeets for pets, but the neighbors stole them. The baby parakeets were retrieved from a tree that had fallen in the swamp. When they came to the house, there was only hair on their bodies. I recalled feeding them by hand with soft bread and milk. They grew into adult parrots that called my name and spoke in clear sentences.

As a girl growing up in this third world country, I was taught how to plant a garden for food. I was taught how to recognize various healing plants, how to cook, and how to care for a home. I was taught how to shop at the market and how to respect the neighbors. But most of all, I was taught that I must have an education.

Education was a major requirement for my grandmother. She insisted on education in the home. I seldom missed a day of school, even when I was ill. I was given some concoction to drink and sent off to school.

There was little to no churchgoing. Occasionally, someone from a neighboring church would invite me to church. On those rare occasions, my grandmother would allow me to attend. I never saw her attend a church, but she would often mention that she grew up under the "Roman Catholic" religion. She would sometimes recite the Hail Mary prayer. So, I learned a little of that prayer from her.

I attended an Anglican school which also had Catholic connotations. It was not until I entered the United States that I became a follower of the Seventh Day Adventist religion.

I am the woman I am today because my grandmother left the legacy of her character within me. Mothers and grandmothers, speak to your daughters and your sons; tell them the stories of your roots. Such were the beginnings of the sand in my shell.

There comes a point when a girl becomes a woman. One might believe this is the time when her body gives the indications of womanhood. I want to give a different analogy for this picture. Sometimes, it takes certain drastic changes in a female's life for her to realize she has entered her rite of passage into womanhood—that is, a woman of substance and of direction. She becomes free; she finds herself, the lover in her, Jesus, and the directing Holy Spirit. She embraces all that she desires from life, and when obstacles encircle her, she creates another path.

Today, I want to say that I have not fully arrived; however, I am closer than when I began. I have moved away from the borders that often tempted to draw me back into a worldly life—a life that was not kind to my survival.

I was called to serve God during my teenage years and after the birth of my first child. Looking back, I realize God always sought ways to save and keep me. Despite the various challenges and disappointments in my life, I have no desire to turn back. My destiny is in front, not behind. I have come too far to turn back. There is no vision in the rear, only a trail of humble beginnings.

Regardless of the pains and the hurts, there is no way we can correct all our wrongs to make them right. However, you can have the desire to tread softly as you create new paths in life.

I am a woman now, and I am holding on to my Creator for dear life. Rather, He is holding me because I am not strong enough to hold Him. I am finally free, free…all praises to my Creator.

EMBRACE ME, LORD

You are a woman, realize your beauty!

A woman with purpose

You are soft, caress yourself, and inhale your essence

You are Spirit, and soul, marvelously constructed

You are strength, strong for life's trials

You are phenomenal; grow with your disappointments

You are joy, share it

Smile with your world…Someone needs to embrace your spirit

You are Loved; Your Lord had inscribed it within

Take your time…Patience enhances your talents

You are Life, live…

Extend your hand…Embrace your Lord

Lay your head on His shoulders; let him carry you.

When you can't hold Him anymore, ask Him to hold you

You are woman. Love it!

You bring sweet aroma to your planet

Even the thorns appreciate holding you up

You are woman, born to create new life

Embrace your Lord; He is your defender, your protector, and your shield

He is the line to supplying a constant flow of never-ending love

You are woman, aren't you proud of her?

Esther C. Nurse

Chapter 2

I KNOW WHO HOLDS MY HAND

I am grateful that my Father the Creator has been holding my hand. Although He has been holding my hand, along the way I stopped to touch, to feel, to utilize all of my senses...basically to do my own thing. During what I want to call my wonder years, my Heavenly Father waited patiently. I am grateful that love is a committed decision to care for, to protect and claim that which is His. 1Cor 13: 4:7: "Love suffers long and is kind; love does not envy; love does not parade itself, is not puffed up; does not behave rudely, does not seek its own, is not provoked, thinks no evil; does not rejoice in iniquity, but rejoices in the truth; bears all things, believes all things, hopes all things, endures all things" (NKJV). Such is the love that is afforded all of us if we all would trust Him with our lives.

Countless times, I ignored His voice. There were times I could clearly hear Him say, "Come on, child, I don't want you to linger here. Keep your focus on me. I will not let go of your hand. I know where you need to be and I will take you there. Allow me to guide you every step of the way." I could hear Him saying, "I know the desires of your heart. I know your spirit. Stand by me and it will be well with your soul." These were the voice I heard and the conversations I ignored.

Have you ever observed a stubborn little child who can hardly handle herself, pulling away from mother or father only to fall hard?

Then, you guessed it: the child has no other choice but to run to the parent to be soothed. Children must learn the hard way. I believe, unknowingly, I was such a child.

Nothing works when your eye is on the Heavenly Father and the other is on your own tasks or your own plan. It strains the eyes, and soon the focus is drawn to the object with the most gravitational pull. If someone wants to lead you away from the person holding your hand, then that person must pull. Often, if you have not anchored your hold, then your hand begins to slip away. Let Jesus hold your hand, and He will also be your anchor.

Imagine with me the paths I have taken—no vain regrets, only reflections. As I traveled along the path or gauntlet of life, it was as if there were diversions on both sides, even though I knew there was a focal point for the journey's completion. I deviated to explore what my eyes desired, succumbing to temptations and sexual sins.

I was introduced to intimacy at a very young age. This was the beginning of my adventure into a world that chipped away at my innocence.

Inexperienced with the world and its enticements, I became a teenage mother as I explored a world that imprisoned my innocence. I was unprepared for what the world presented. I thought love was the cheesecake of life. I was in love with being in love and thought everyone felt that way. So, I became entangled in a web of deceptive relationships that promised love, only to find a harsh reality of emotional abuse and mental anguish.

I became pregnant at seventeen years old. I graduated from high school while I was six months pregnant. One month after my eighteenth birthday, I was a mother. My future to many seemed bleak.

My parents were disappointed. Not to mention, my mother was also pregnant at the same time. I was living in a home with few conversations and interactions with my mother. I stayed in my room, only venturing out when everyone had turned in, because I was ashamed, but mostly ashamed because my parents were ashamed of me. I had done a bad thing.

I knew little about pregnancy. I knew little about what was happening to me. There were times the baby would move, and I could see his bone sticking out my side. I was so afraid, I did not dare tell anyone.

I can recall the day I told my mother I was pregnant. I wrote her a three-page letter. Since we did not talk much, this was my best approach. I just knew something bad was going to happen: Either I would get a beating, or I would be put out of the house. I had to take my chances.

So, I sat nervously on my bed while she read the letter. My mother's words to me were, "Are you going to keep it? Did you go to the doctor? What did you think I was going to do?" My reply was, "Put me out." That was the expected recourse. I was relieved when the anticipated recourse did not happen.

The night my baby was born, I had been in labor for eleven hours, and again I found myself alone. No mother to hold my hand, and no baby father by my side. He was with his other girl.

I recalled one of my teachers, who esteemed me with a potential to be successful, said, "You have ruined my life." While all of my classmates prepared for college classes, I prepared for the care of my new son.

Looking back today, I believe I somehow beat the odds. Another testimony of God's goodness, grace, and mercy towards me. My refinement had begun, and I was oblivious. 1 Peter 1:7: "That the trial of your faith (being much more precious than gold that perisheth, though it be tested with fire) might be found unto praise and honor and glory at the appearing of Jesus Christ" (NIV).

During the time I was raising my son, the crack epidemic had started. The New York City building where I lived became infested with marijuana and crack sales. There were repeated police raids; even persons who seemed untouchable succumbed to the drug epidemic. Not because of any one special thing, but I was determined to save my son from the streets. I needed to do something that would protect both of us.

It was then that the Lord called me. I was called to join a church. At the time, I was the only member of my family attending church.

As a result of my dedication to attend church alone with my baby, my family also began to follow.

I became instrumental in seeing my entire family joining the church and becoming Seventh Day Adventists. Along the way, God sent several special people into my life; these people helped me care for myself and my child. The first blessing was the greatest babysitter. She was a woman who was born in the southern parts of the United States. She and her husband had four children. At least, three of her children were not productive. When she saw me and my baby, she said, "I will help you because you are trying to do something for yourself." This woman cared for my son as if he was her own grandchild.

With babysitting secured, I was able to enter college the year after the birth of my son. I was determined to succeed. I was told I would have to finish college in five years as I was so behind. Suffice it to say, I finished college in four years while working two jobs and caring for my son.

The son I chose to carry is now a doctor, with accolades of three master's degrees and a doctoral degree. All my dreams are not fully realized, but I can safely say it was my Heavenly Father's grace.

There is a saying that the eyes see and desire more than the stomach can withstand. In other words, as you go on your journey, there is much to distract. On one side of the path you take, let's say you pick up some yellow flowers. A way off, you pick up some rocks, stop to idle; then as you continue, you might stop to rest, and so on.

In your idleness, you find yourself thinking you are alone, so you lose focus and begin to wander off. Your wandering might be to follow a friend or a lover, a career or children or money, you name it. Before you realize it, you have strayed off the path and your way becomes a wilderness, a barren land, a place of danger with many attacks from the enemy.

Seemingly, there is no way out. Even in the midst of this, God is still declaring His love for you. There is an excellent reminder, according to 2 Corinthians 10:12: "For we dare not class ourselves or compare ourselves with those who commend themselves. But they measuring themselves by themselves, and comparing themselves among themselves, are not wise" (NKJV). God wants you to understand that He is the center of your joy, and He holds the answers to all your questionings.

Someone once told me that if you linger near the borders, it is easy to be lured back to the other side. That is the life you once led. But if you move away from the borders, the chances of being lured back to the other side diminishes.

There is a delightful conversation that God had with His people. In Leviticus 23:22: "When you reap the harvest of your land, you shall not wholly reap the corners of your field when you reap, nor shall you gather any gleaning from your harvest. You shall leave them for the poor and for the stranger: I am the Lord your God" (NKJV). God wants to take care of you, in addition to those who are on the borders.

There is no need to travel to the borders because He has given us all that is in the center of the fields. He dwells in the center of our lives, providing for all of our needs. The point is not to be idle near the borders. Someone is holding your hand. Believe that even in times when you fall, someone is still holding your hand. Why do we choose to play tug-of-war with God? Your hands are too tiny to tug on mighty hands. Because we are babes in God's sight, we are spared many disasters because He yearns to save us.

Subsequently, I was blessed with two other children. Again, I encountered severe emotional trauma on the day that two of my children—for whom I bent over backwards, who I loved deeply—told me I was not their choice. They no longer wanted to reside with me. One after the other, they left my home.

For nine years, I had no contact with them. I had moved to another state during this traumatic time, and I even got a large three-bedroom duplex apartment, hoping they would return to me, and I readied preparations for them. That never happened. Again, I was alone.

Eighteen years of court hearings, loss of all my finances, and aloneness led me to finally realize I did not walk alone. Feeling disconnected with despair creeping into the slow shape of a circle was when I realized that my Creator wanted me to walk beside Him in His harmony.

For the journey to be completed and His plan materialized, He had to continue holding my hand, and I had to want Him to take the entire burden.

I believe I have always had a stubborn streak within—or perhaps an explorative streak. I suppose that came from embracing a desire to be my own protector. Because my Creator knew that, all the lessons I learned were the ones He allowed. This was because He wanted me to understand… When I thought I was in control, He was in control.

He created me and He knows everything about me. When I pursued love, He said wait. It felt like my wait would never end. In instances when I took matters into my own hand, I still heard His voice: Wait. Can you believe I'm still waiting? Each time I pursued my own aspiration, His scolding became stronger and the consequences harsher. And each time my heart cried, He continued holding my hand.

I hear His voice clearly…. His spirit speaks with force yet with love that warms the soul. "You are my daughter. You don't know the plans I have for your life, but if I allow you to continue this path with you leading, you will not make it…. If you would allow me, I will lead you to higher heights."

I heard Him saying,

"Now that you have lost everything, you have no money, and you have found yourself in a ditch, stretch out your hand….

"I will not only lift you out, but I will fill your life to overflowing….

"Keep your focus on me and your feet will travel the distance….

"I will not allow the stones to hinder the journey….

"The distractions on the side of the road will not disappear, but as you keep your focus on me, the obstacles will only be a blur, disappearing in your periphery."

The Creator wants to hold your hand. Isn't it time that you allow the Creator to hold your hand? The hold will be a stronger bond. Don't let go! He needs to know that you trust Him and believe in His promises. Sight will not be necessary because He will also be your sight. He will carry you all the way.

Imagine you have blindfolds, and the only hand you can rely on is the one that holds you. Imagine that your feet are planted firmly on the ground, and there is no need to worry about your steps because you feel confidence with every step. You feel yourself nearing your destination, you feel yourself being delivered, because He who holds your hand is strong and your trust is sure.

You are finally ready to experience the freedom of being the woman or man you were meant to be. If only you had known that life could be so blissful the moment you surrendered and allowed the Creator to hold your hand.

WHEN THE SPIRIT SPEAKS

I hear the Spirit speaking

Time to take your place time to shed the fear, chains,
anger, jealousy, and all those negative spirits that
have kept you bound for so many years

A man is not what you need but power beyond all power

I hear the Spirit speaking

It's time to take over

My place is with you

You have no room for anything else

I will fulfill all your dreams and aspiration

All your desires, I have examined, and I am now ready
to take my place within the cavity of your soul

My gift is to give you all the joy you have desired

I am about to unleash the essence of you

Your light is about to shine

You are shining already

You do not have to settle for anything

You are a Queen

Nothing happens by chance

You have been chosen to be Royalty

The great one has only been preparing you

Your time has come to take your place on your throne

I hear the Spirit speaking

You are a Queen, and the world awaits your entrance

I will be there to advise, uphold you, to continue your tutoring

You are my Queen, and your King awaits your entry

I hear the Spirit speaking

Oh, great Queen arise; the time has come for you to take your place

Silence now…

Here comes the Queen

Esther C. Nurse

Chapter 3

FINDING PEACE WITHIN THE STORM

One of my favorite poems is "Desiderata." My favorite lines are:

Go placidly amid the noise and haste, and remember what peace there may be in silence.... Speak your truth quietly and clearly; and listen to others, even the dull and the ignorant; they too have their story.... Therefore, be at peace with God, whatever you conceive Him to be. And whatever your labors and aspirations in the noisy confusion of life, keep peace with your soul.

When I think of these words, I have a greater appreciation for nature: the changes that take place, the sounds of the wind, the musical rushing of a stream, or the thunderous roar of a waterfall. I am given a conscious glimpse of the plan of life that our Creator had for His children.

I can feel His presence even in the softest gentle breeze, yet there is silence even in the softness of the wind. It is as if peace gives a spiritual kiss, toying with the senses and playing a gentle game that relaxes and soothes even during the worst of storms. Nature rages in a cocktail mix of anger, debris, and confusion.

Such is the case with our lives at times. It is amazing how nature mimics the patterns of our lives, yet we take no precaution to protect ourselves. There are those who refuse to realize the care that has been predetermined to shelter the mind from unexpected destruction.

Observe a bird on a limb during a storm. He clasps his tiny feet around the branch and holds on to that limb as the storm rages on. After the storm is over, you can observe that same bird whistling a tune as if there had never been a storm. The key… hold on! How deep is your faith?

Mothers, fathers, daughters, sons, sisters, brothers: Hold on for dear life. Right there in your storm is a vine. The vine is connected to strong roots, not planted by ordinary hands. The vine dresser is our Heavenly Father. Uprooting is virtually impossible unless you let go. Deliverance comes directly within your storm.

There is a saying: "When a child is born, the parents should cry because of the world that that child must now enter and is expected to grow up, and hopefully enter adulthood." The saying goes on to expound that when a person dies, there should be celebration because the drudgery of life for that person has now ended. They enter into a sleep that life can never replicate. When you realize that you are a child of the King, you can smile at death, trials, and disappointments because you have embraced the Spirit that connects to your soul.

Every child who enters this world has a burden to bear and a final appointment with death. Anyone experiencing death in the family, either for the first or however many times, will experience a feeling of utter destruction and a lack of calm that no comfort seems able to blot out. This death does not have to be the loss of life; it may include the loss of relationships, children, career, and so much else. These are storms that only a strong connection to the source of life can alleviate.

I know of women who have encountered the loss of a child, a marriage relationship, or any love relationship. Because of these disappointments, they have not allowed themselves to return to a life of normalcy. A friend of mine lost her son to gunfire. She said, "I asked God to spare his life, but God did not." She felt disappointed, lost, and unvindicated. She felt she had no one to trust, not even God. I say, "Find peace in all of your sorrowful disappointments."

As a woman who seemingly has been on a quest for love and to be loved for my entire life, I have faced the reality of expectations that became disappointments, of insults and crude tauntings from the love I just knew would be the love of my life, until Jesus came. These were relationships I had chosen. The key is: I did not allow God to choose. Instead, I felt it and so it must have been the right decision.

Reflecting on my life, I remember several incidents of disappointment that would on occasion cause me to cringe when I think I was actually involved in these situations. One such occasion was the night my first child was born. I was alone, I was scared. I had led a sheltered life and knew nothing about childbirth or what was happening to me. To top that, the father of the child was at the home of another woman, while I was in agony and fear. I was a teenage mother, caring for a baby. I was alone. I had no job. I was a recent high school graduate and living in a home with disappointed parents. This was only a small portion of the many disappointments and storms that would follow over the years.

As a young woman living on my own and trusting that the people I encountered were those who cared, I was taught one of life's most hurtful lessons. I think of King Solomon advising his son about an immoral woman. He told his son that her ways would lead to death.

Here is another one of my traumas. How about returning to your home to find the interior completely demolished? Decorations destroyed, bedroom devastated, all your personal papers gone. Moreover, the man who did all this damage called nightly to read pages of your diary, then laughed. I was a naïve young lady who trusted the man in my life with the keys to my home. The reason for the destruction was jealousy. I was unprepared to deal with the consequences I was now enduring. No one should have been able to violate my space or my spirit.

I was a young lady with no direction or sense of how the world would not be kind to my innocence. I did not know what it was like to have a father's advice or protection. I did not know that there was a God who loves me, who was protecting me, who saw all I was going through, and who knew my end from my beginning.

I lived with constant threats of police reports, court appearances, death threats, and stalking. I am glad that I am a strong believer in the saying, "This too shall pass." Today, I am grateful for the presence of the Holy Spirit in my life. He would not allow me to succumb to the vicissitudes of life.

Storms sometimes pass through for brief moments, while some linger, leaving huge destruction. Others pass over as warnings. Nevertheless, life continues, and everyone cleans up to start over. Somehow, I managed to endure all of the storms without mental breakdown. I am still enduring storms. I suppose there will always be a storm.

Despite all of my storms, I am seen as the one with strength. I was always the person in the family who was contacted in times of disasters or strange happenings in the lives of my siblings. In some way, I am considered the storm wall. When a family member got into legal trouble, the police called me. When there was a death, I received the call first.

These are the times when you begin to feel as if you are standing in the eye of the storm while everyone else has found a safe haven. Little did I know that the eye of the storm is the safe place. There are times when you will feel that all the arrows are aimed at and directed only for you. How do you remain sane in the midst of all your storms? Reach out your hand and ask the power above to hold your hand. Remind yourself of Psalms 107:29: "He maketh the storm a calm, so that the waves thereof are still." And Psalms 34:17-20: "[The righteous] cry, and the LORD heareth, and delivereth them out of all their troubles."

It is tempting to distinguish between the fate of the male child and the female child, but that would be unfair. When a child is born, his or her mother feels the sting of new life as the mother's body goes through the trauma of pressure, contraction, and detachment. Yet the mother seldom remembers the pain after the birth of her child. The mother may recall there was pain, but she seldom can reach out to that spot to recall any recurring pain. She finds a sensual peace and relief after the ordeal has ended. Sometimes we do not realize when our storms have ended. We just know that we begin to rejoice and testify to God's goodness after we have come through a storm.

It is said that the safest place is in the eye of the storm. The eye of the storm is the only peaceful part of the hurricane. So, if you can consider the storms around raging but sit still, what seemed so frightening and unconquerable will eventually lull into a distant soft breeze. Seeking to get through the eye wall is the dangerous part, as there is too much debris and definitely a possibility of not surviving the turbulence. The center of low pressure in the storm is the eye. The lower the central pressure, the fiercer the storm and the higher the winds. Nevertheless, the eye itself is calm and peaceful. It is no wonder we are admonished to "Be still and know that our God is God" (KJV). There is no storm that He will not see us through, with ease. That includes the storm of death, broken family, loss of finances, health challenges, loss of employment, fires, broken heart, lost marriages, lost children, and on and on. Be still!

THE FIGHT FOR MY LIFE

The battle is fierce!!

On this side, the face of evil; on that side, the face of evil

Behind the face of evil

How did you find yourself in this place?

Surrounded!!

No chance to escape

Except up!!

I have never seen a battle won with the victims leaving upward

This battle has no relief fighters

Yet you have survived all these years

The pains of the blows are beginning to take their toll

The feet no longer able to hold up the body

Yet the knees indicate their strength

Use me! I will get you through this

Even though there is no place to go but up

Despair has turned to fear

Fear to the loss of hope

How come no one has come to the assistance?

Is the world empty of help?

Is there a prize if they take the body?

What good is a body without a spirit?

I can't even watch!

The Spirit is helpless without its body

If the spirit escapes upward, it is doomed
to gaze upon its destroyed host

I am told many battles are won on the knees

What an awkward position to be in when
the enemy has you surrounded

No time to think of purpose

But then you look up allowing the spirit to escape

With tear-filled eyes, an audience has gathered

The spirit is ushered upward

Yet there remains strength in your knees

The battle is not over, the body has not succumbed

The fight continues, but when does it end?

Stand with me, I am still on my knees

I close my eyes

Help must be on the way for me,

I am still on my knees

Help must be on its way

The battle is raging....

Esther C. Nurse

Chapter 4

THE SEASON OF NEW CHALLENGES

What to Do?

December 31st, 2017, would be a pivotal turning point in my life. I was never a sickly child or adult. Never had any major illnesses, except for the occasional common cold. Generally, these colds would be swiftly taken care of with some cultural bush medicines or home remedies. My motto, however, is "lemon and honey"—the treatment I raised my children on, and now they are doing the same with their children. I did not always know what to do, however; more times than I can count, I was Spirit-led to administer the correct medicinal intervention. I can only attribute this to guidance from the Holy Spirit.

Nothing, however, could prepare me for what I was going to have to embrace. I was about to embark on my Job-like experience (Job from the bible). The devil would attack me on all fronts. He attacked my little family first.

I suddenly found myself without the love and voice of my children. While they did not die, the devil separated me from contact with two of my children for nine years. For twenty-six years, I was a single parent, raising my children with the little I had, sending them to church school, sacrificing my own happiness so that all would be well with them.

I did not date, I did not go out except to church. I worked, came home from work, cooked, cleaned, assisted with homework, took them on outings and back to church again. That was my life. While I longed for help and a relationship, I was not willing to sacrifice my children's happiness. I did not want anyone to abuse my children. My thoughts would not be pure should any of my children be ill-treated because of my need for companionship.

As a result of my years of sacrifices and putting my children on a pedestal, they were to have the best and be the best. I became socially awkward. I am still that way and am often misunderstood by those who approach me. I remember a pastor telling me once that if I ever wanted to be in a relationship, I should act dumb because I portrayed too strong a personality. Imagine that. The Holy Spirit has not afforded me the wisdom of how to be the perfect dummy. Proverbs 4:7: "Wisdom is the principal thing; therefore, get wisdom: and with all thy getting get understanding" (KJV). Let no one take away the innate blessings that God has imparted to you.

Imagine my surprise when the children I loved so deeply and to whom I dedicated my life were no longer in my life. I recall the day I realized that my family as I knew it would be dismantled.

It was a Sabbath (Saturday) morning, and I decided that I and my children would walk to church instead of taking the bus. It was summer and the morning was a comfortable warmth, so that walking would not leave us sweaty upon our arrival to church.

My three children were well dressed and well groomed. The boys wore their ties and well-ironed shirts and pants. My daughter was in a lovely dress, her hair in place as she liked it. My children walked in front while I lingered behind them, not too far so that I could swoop in and cover them should there be any noticeable danger. I was just admiring the closeness of the children as they walked together, looking so well. I was proud. *Look at them*, I thought, *these three are mine*.

Suddenly I heard a voice almost audibly speaking in my head: "Things are not going to be the same."

The devil in swift, repetitive, deliberate, calculative movements snatched my little lambs. My quiet middle son suddenly wanted to be in the home of a father he barely knew. My daughter would follow two years later. My elder son would leave to travel the world. My family was broken and, again, I was alone.

Then my finances were attacked. I found myself working, but all of my checks were taken away each time I got paid. I was constantly in court with the father of the children. There was always some petition being filed for something.

I eventually found myself broke and alone in a strange state. I had no friends where I lived, and at one point I had no transportation.

In some strange way, I want to believe the Lord had been preparing me for the lonely adult years ever since I was a child. I could see biblical references for my life at every turn. My new apartment was situated near a creek, I could see the mountains that surrounded the area of my residence. There were lush trees outside the front door of my beautiful duplex apartment.

I was broke, with very few funds in the bank and with a three-bedroom apartment while I waited for my children to come home. Suffice it to say, I never spent a day on the streets. Somehow, I always found the money to pay the rent on time. I worked two part-time jobs. There was always a place I could go to pick up some food. At one point, I was able to receive public assistance. Like Elijah, the Lord had brought me out of a big city to a house near a creek—I called it my brook—until it was time for me to move on. Eventually, I ended up owning my own home. That is another testimony.

With all that I had gone through, though, the devil was not satisfied. He decided to touch my health. Isn't it good to know a God who can give approval to have his children's lives touched in such a way that the devil still cannot end it?

On December 31st, 2017, I went to the hospital, reeling from severe abdominal pain. I had been having acid reflux nightly; I must have drunk every antacid known to man, not to mention home remedies. Nothing was helping. I began burping the foulest odors, but I still did not have it checked out.

I was determined to cure myself. I had always done that and recovered nicely. But the pain became so unbearable that my only choice was to visit the hospital. I recall the day was extremely cold, and I needed to cover the outside pipes of my house. I was initially at a dinner get-together, so I thought, while in severe pain, that I needed to take care of the pipes first before I go to the hospital. I had no idea of the seriousness of my condition. I left the get-together, drove about ten to twelve miles home, and then another seventeen miles to the hospital.

Upon arriving at the hospital, I was sent for an MRI. Everyone who entered my room seemed somehow sheepish about not wanting to address my concerns about what was happening. Each person would say the nurse practitioner would be in soon. Finally, he arrived. He said, "We don't know what is happening, but we cannot see your stomach. We will have to admit you."

I was admitted, but I would not be able to get any results because it was New Year's Eve and New Year's Day. On the third day, while my niece braided my hair, a doctor walked into my hospital room. He said he was an oncologist. He said, "We are not sure what is happening. We believe it is cancer. We will not know anything due to the holidays. You will be scheduled for an endoscopy."

Staring at the doctor with a somewhat get-out-of-here look, I responded with subtle sarcasm, "Don't worry, I don't have cancer."

He left. I was then prepped for more tests. This was the beginning of my long journey of being prodded and probed. The first Gastroenterologist could not see anything in my stomach. I was told I would have to wait for another more experienced Gastroenterologist —the best of the best. Indeed, he was. I was again put to sleep. This doctor went along my stomach wall to reach the bottom of my stomach. The news then came: "You have a large tumor." It was about to join the other side of my stomach.

Imagine having a tumor so large that the doctors said it was acting like a bridge. All of my food was resting on this bridge, unable to pass adequately into the intestines.

I did not understand because my body seemed to be functioning normally. There was no hindrance in bowel movements. I was able to eat and feel full, never with any regurgitation, except I began having the foulest burps. Still, I did not check this out. At night, I slept sitting up.

The pain and acid reflux were unbearable. Still, I thought my condition trivial. It seems there was only a little crevice remaining that allowed liquids to pass. I was told the tumor was bleeding, it was as hard as a rock. A biopsy would be taken.

While still in the recovery room after my endoscopy, I was approached by two very young surgeons. They appeared so young, they could have been my sons. In my grogginess, I said to the one who spoke first, "You are so young." The young doctor introduced himself and said, "You appear to have a very serious case, but we will take care of you."

The young doctor was saying the right words for the situation. I could hear the two surgeons discussing with the Gastroenterologist what would be the best course. All three appeared extremely puzzled, it was a case they had never seen before. I observed their searching eyes. Even their physique spoke of the enigma that was mine and mine alone. With much uncertainty, the young surgeon asked something of the endocrinologist, who responded. "You might just have to pulverize it." The young surgeon looked over at me. I believe they thought I was asleep and still under the influence of anesthesia.

I just closed my eyes. No emotions. I could not comprehend… My situation was serious. Somehow, I sheltered myself from the ugliness of my true illness. The doctors' faces appeared so searching yet so unassuming. The only comfort that came to my mind was that the young doctor was very handsome. I smiled, closed my eyes, and continued to rest.

I spent seven days in the hospital before I received any results. Finally, the oncologist came back. **Cancer**. He outlined, nonchalantly, that the cancer had not perforated the stomach, so he labeled my condition Stage I. I now had Stage I stomach cancer. He said I would have to go through several weeks of chemo, and I was to see him at his office upon my discharge. After chemo, I would have surgery. Then there would be multiple appointments to endure.

I was faced with a circumstance to which I had never been exposed before. I was a woman who was never ill. Now I had an illness that made up for all the illnesses I never had.

I questioned myself. "What is this cancer anyway?" I had heard of it, but it was not for me. It was a condition that happened to people I heard about. From what I knew, just hearing the word "cancer" was apparently a death sentence. When you tell anyone you have cancer, you can see how they look at you with deep sadness or despair.

The only thing I could think to ask the oncologist was, "Am I going to lose my hair?" He said yes.... Somehow, I was not concerned about the cancer, I was more concerned about my hair. I had been growing my hair naturally for seven years, and I loved the versatility of the styles I could do naturally. I did not want to lose my hair.

At that moment, I believe God had allowed me to absorb the shock by turning my attention to my hair. Thinking back, what a vain response I had, when just the diagnosis of cancer sends chills down anyone's spine. My specific case was so serious that the surgeon said, "You do not understand what a sick woman you are."

Indeed, I did not understand. I did not want to understand. This was not happening. How was I going to get married now? What would happen to all the beautiful things I had envisioned for myself? No, I was not accepting the thought of cancer.

My sister was present at the time of the original news. She said, "We will get you a nice wig." I did not want a wig; I wanted my hair. As the weeks went on, I was placed on a liquid diet for about two months, nothing but protein shakes. To this day, just looking at the box of a protein shake makes me quiver. I detest the drink. I had tried every brand name and every flavor. My surgeon suggested a specific brand, the one he used. That did not help. I was not a happy camper; I had no choice but to endure. Either I obeyed or the consequences would not be in my best interest.

I recall during my months of chemo and liquid diet that I was so sick at the time. All I could do was lie in bed daily. Not to be morbid, but my only thoughts at times were: If the chemo did not kill me, the diarrhea would. One day after several bouts with the commode, I was almost ready to throw in my proverbial towel. I lay on my bed and prayed just one sentence: "Lord, what is going to happen to me?" I rested my head on my pillow. I knew I was not asleep when I heard a voice say, "You are going to be okay." I almost believed someone was in my house. I even opened my eyes and looked around. I knew I was alone. Where was this voice coming from? On that day, I was able to rest better than on the other days.

About two to three weeks after I began chemo, I began to have hair loss. I recall having my hair in cornrows, all braided backwards. One day, I lifted every braid off my head. I was now balder than a Siamese cat. I found it difficult to look at myself in the mirror. I would pass by a mirror, looking cross-eyed, with quick glances. I could not recognize the person in the mirror. She was a stranger.

Since it was the winter, I wore a hat on the rare occasions I left the house. I could not easily go out because I did not know when I would need to rush to the commode. I was cold and lonely. I spent my days in bed or, when I could hold up my head, watching television.

Some days, I could not make it to my kitchen to eat something. I was dizzy and fearful I would fall. I called no one, and no one visited me. A friend from New York called a woman who was practicing medical missionary.

This woman was willing to travel from her home, two hours away, to stay with me once a month on weekends. She administered some of her remedies: lemon water, a red-light lamp which she illuminated on the area of my stomach. She helped me tidy my home, changed my sheets, and prepared some breakfast. She attempted a regimen of exercise, sunlight, and documented eating habits.

Most of the time, I was too weak to get out of bed. She escorted me to the laundromat on days when I felt strong enough. She did all that she could in the short time we spent together. We worshipped together on the mornings she was at the house. At times, she seemed to become angry when I did not retreat to my room to read something biblical.

At the time, my head could not focus on anything. I was not in the best frame of mind or strength to even read my bible. She assisted me for a couple of months. When I had surgery, she returned to assist me with bathing as I had a drainage tube attached to my stomach. I was at times embarrassed to have another woman helping me. I needed help, but my pride was interfering. I am grateful that God knew my need and provided. He sent a stranger who spent her time and her money to assist me. I am grateful for her. Great is my Father's faithfulness.

Suffice it to say, I pulled through and had my surgery. Half of my stomach was removed. This was only after pleading to not have a bariatric type of surgery. My surgeon said I would be getting a bariatric surgery for the price of one. Bariatric surgery is a procedure where the stomach is reduced to the size of an egg. This surgery is usually done for persons who are morbidly obese. He was suggesting this would aid in my weight loss.

I could not see myself as he did. I did not want the image he was portraying. He said I would be thinner than I was, but I could attend support groups with others who had gone through similar surgeries. He said I was going to like my new body appearance as I began to lose the weight.

I was not listening to him. I pleaded that he do all he could to save my stomach and he should explain to me afterwards what he did. He seemed a little perturbed (surgeons enjoy cutting). His response was "We will see when we get in there." Later, he said, "You are lucky. I left more of your stomach than I usually do." I suppose one could respond here with the question: Was he doing me a favor? But why argue when I was grateful for my life?

At the time, I could only see myself as a crippled woman, not one that would be seemingly cured of my tumor or cancer. I saw myself as half of a woman. I was in mental turmoil. At first, I interpreted the surgery as one in which they would remove my stomach, remove the infected area, and return my stomach—much like removing the heart, working on it, and replacing it. But that was not the case. I cannot describe the loneliness I felt. I did not have the support of any family in my home, and my friends all lived in different states. How was I going to survive this ordeal alone?

I would be well for two years, no incidents. I returned to work after five months of recovering. I had succeeded in getting through what was my death sentence. I was given a second chance. God had a plan about which I had no idea. "What was required of me?" "How was my life different from others who had had a similar health condition?" I recalled when I told my mother of my condition, she began to cry. She said, "Something terrible has happened to you. I have treated patients with your condition, and they did not survive." I remember responding, "Mommy, I'm going to be okay." I believed in my mind there was no real register of how serious my condition was. I treated the situation as if it was a common cold. Somehow, my mind would not allow me to rest on this condition.

In October of 2020, I began experiencing extreme lethargic episodes. I was willing myself to get out of bed and do menial chores. It was as if I had run a ten-mile race just walking from the bed to the bathroom.

I then began to notice some yellowing of my eyes. Again, I dismissed it as the reflection of the bathroom light. This is God's mercy. My blessings cannot be interpreted at times, except with a hallelujah praise. The psalmist David said in Psalm 124:7: "Our soul is escaped as a bird out of the snare of the fowlers: the snare is broken, and we are escaped" (KJV).

My urine was a lovely shade of brown. I thought it was because I was not drinking enough water. It was the devil determined to take me out. My liver was now under attack. But as Donnie McClurkin sang, "Not Yet."

I was reluctant to go to my doctor. Then one day in November of 2020, while I was at work, I saw that the urine color still had not changed even after drinking much water. I decided to see my primary care doctor. I left work that afternoon and was immediately admitted to the hospital. The diagnosis: Jaundice. A stent was put into my liver to deal with a blockage.

I was later asked to report to my oncologist. The news worsened. He said the hospital MRI showed that my cancer had returned. At first, he said it was in a duct within my liver. Then he said more tests needed to be done. The next test results then returned: cancer of the peritoneum.

What was the peritoneum? I never heard of it. I began my own research. Then discouragement set in. The internet showed me gruesome depictions of different types of peritoneal cancers. This thin lining of the stomach I imagined could not sustain me. My heart was faint. I read the survival rate of a person with this condition. The doctor was right:

one year at most. What was I to do? That isolated, abandoned spirit came upon me again. It was not the thought of death. It was a feeling of despair. Who was I going to talk to about this? The one male friend I had I no longer trusted.

I contacted my brother's fiancée and said, "This does not look good for me." Her reply to me was "Stay off the internet and trust God." There it was—reassurance in the midst of despair.

I now had a hemlock in my side for the liver. Somehow the hospital had forgotten to attach a drainage bag and I did not know that I needed one. I was sitting in the oncologist's office with new news. I had both a jaundice problem and a cancer problem. The devil was really going to get me this time.

I said to my oncologist, "What are you saying to me?" He said I now had Stage IV stomach cancer. "You have twelve months to live." I believe I said something like "Hell." "What did you say?" he asked. I said, "Nothing." Somehow, I believe he expected a different reaction.

Perhaps he expected tears, sadness, pleading for help, hollering and screaming. I'm not sure. I want to believe that doctors have become so desensitized because they have had to relay bad news to their patients so often that certain reactions are naturally expected. In some morbid way, I want to believe they enjoy seeing this depressed reaction.

Instead, my reaction stunned him. I was calm. I said nothing else, except to his assistant: "Where do you want me to go now?" I was told to head to my scheduled treatment. I left the office and retreated to the back of the building where I would receive my regular treatment.

I felt so alone, sitting in the office of a doctor who had just placed a short leash on my life expectancy. Who could I talk to? My son was aware of my appointment, so I called him and revealed what the doctor said. He did not take the news well. He called his wife, who called me. Both had agreed within split seconds of my contact that I would go to New York for a second opinion.

My brother and his fiancée both worked in oncology at a reputable New York hospital. They secured for me one of the best doctors in the city. I later learned she was not an easy doctor to obtain and very sought after. Let me tell you, she was an extremely attractive woman. When I saw her, all I could say was "You are beautiful." I want to shout because through the ugliness of cancer, God allowed me to be surrounded by beautiful people who wanted to help me. Every person I met at that hospital wanted to do something special for me. I was blessed. Not to mention that it was so well organized that I received transportation to and from the hospital for every visit.

I recalled feeling extremely nervous informing my current oncologist that I was seeking a second opinion. On the morning of my appointment with him, I prayed continually, fearful of his reaction. In some way, I had imagined he would say, "What do you need another opinion for? I already told you: You have a short time to live." So, I sat in his office, nervously awaiting his entry. I said in the softest voice, "Doctor, my son wants me to get a second opinion in New York."

To my surprise, he said, "I want you to get one." Did I hear correctly? Color returned to my face. He asked, "Do you have a hospital in mind? I can recommend one." I was happy to inform him I had a doctor already waiting for me. He said he would forward my files to the new doctor. Wow! This was easier than I could have imagined. I left his office feeling overjoyed. I was released to travel.

But the devil was not done with me yet. Remember that hemlock? No drainage bag attached after the stent procedure (a bilirubin drain)? I had been flushing that thing as instructed twice daily, but all of the flushes were going into my body.

I became badly infected. All that should have been draining was returning into my system. I know what you are thinking: Lawsuit! Perhaps I had good reason, but why allow the devil to steal your praise? Every chance you get, give God the glory for your life.

Some sisters from my church happened to visit to assist me. One was my Pastor's wife, and the other was the head deaconess. I was so cold that day. I just could not get warm. I was under two comforters, the central heat was going, and I had a space heater on high. Nothing could warm me. My Pastor's wife made me some tea, but I wanted nothing. She finally said, "Call your doctor. We are going to the hospital."

I first reported to the cancer center, where they took some blood tests, gave me antibiotics, and sent me home. I stayed at home for two or three days—I want to say it was a Tuesday—still not feeling my best. On Friday, I received a call from the oncologist nurse. "Get to the hospital immediately," she said. "You have a very bad bacterial infection." Again, being home alone, I called a family member, indicated what was happening, and left for the hospital.

I was again admitted to the same hospital that did the original stent procedure. No one discussed the missing drainage bag. I recalled being isolated in a room. The cancer center had notified the hospital of their results. A doctor for infectious diseases was called in. I was in a bad way.

They started me on four different antibiotics. My situation was beyond serious. The antibiotics were very strong. They were finally able to find the one that worked. I never complained to anyone.

In December 2020, I finally flew to New York. I was in the heart of the COVID pandemic. I had cancer, a drainage bag attached to my side, and two planes to catch. What a challenge. I want to pause here to say God gets all the glory. The battle is not yours; it is the Lord's. One of my favorite scriptures is found in Exodus 14:14: "The Lord will fight for you, and you will hold your peace" (NKJ). But that is still not my shouting moment. You will shout with me soon.

I spent three months in New York. I was started on immune therapy coupled with chemo. I returned to my home in February 2021. I went to see my oncologist who scheduled me for a PET scan in March.

The day after the scan, I returned to see him. I met with the nurse practitioner instead. She came into the room, stating she had very good news. "What is it?" I asked. She spoke.

"No cancer was found."

NO cancer found!

She sat directly in front of me, I grabbed and squeezed both of her thighs and began to cry. No cancer was found...

I left the office that day, walking on air. Four months after I was told I only had twelve months to live, I would be told no cancer was found. The following month upon my return, I met with my doctor. He explained his amazement. He even showed me on the computer the inactivity of the cancer. His statement to me, "Whatever you are doing, keep doing it." He recommended continued treatments with the doses lowered. According to my oncologist, this type of cancer is subject to return.

I am currently in the process of transitioning to pills. I say, "To God be the glory."

I don't want to use the term "cancer survivor." I believe this term implies an acceptance that death was the only alternative. I chose life. This was something my mother said often while she was in the nursing home: "I want to live." I adopted the same principle: "I want to live." Death is inevitable, but it should not be a choice. Choose life today. God is still in control.

As I am completing this book, I am approaching the one-year mark of my pronounced lease on life. It is now the end of September, 2021. I am not certain when my year began, and what its duration is, but I can only testify that to God be the glory. I'm still here.

I am grateful to a God who knows the end from the beginning and a God who allows the devil to come so far and no further. A God who sits high and looks low. A God who hears the prayers of all his children.

In a world with approximately eight billion people, there is a God who hears my specific petition, who knows all about me, who puts my tears in a bottle, who never leaves me alone. He who knows every hair now growing back on my head. I am his and He is mine. I am truly blessed and have much for which I glorify His name.

CHARITY

I didn't know love was not a feeling

Love was a Principle

It's when the head interprets what the heart wants to say

I didn't know there was a rational explanation

Many love affairs are born because of the passion of the heart

Yet I didn't know how to love

When the words of love spoke in harsh tones

I thought…

How could the voice I hear come from the heart?

Flowers are not charity

I am told, "The glory of man is as a flower in the grass"

This glory of love is only but for a moment

It blooms with passion overnight

It appeals to the eyes in the morning

And the odor is of sensual essence

Then its color fades, its essence evaporates, petals die,

It returns to the grass

If only I understood the Principle of love

Love is everlasting, cultivated by the Creator

Only a chosen few experience its full impact

Teach me charity, teach me its principles

Then I will live eternally

I didn't know charity was in the soul

You are alive because charity experienced death

This breath of life, love beyond compare

Oh, sweet charity, feed me with your essence,

Help me develop your principle

Esther C. Nurse

A BEAUTIFUL SOUL

Breathe on me breath of life

My soul longs to see the color of your form

What is this breath that creates the soul?

Reach into the depths of me,

You'll find a beautiful soul

The light that radiates, like the burning bush

So is a contented soul

As a right spirit is renewed and a clean heart is jubilant

So is your beautiful soul

When man dies, it is said that the soul returns to its Creator

I wonder why the breath of life is so magical

How come I know it is there, and yet I can't harness it?

It's the essence of you

It's your beautiful soul

Esther C. Nurse

Chapter 5

THE SEASON OF ACCEPTANCE AND RESTORATION

These Tired Feet

I thought I would write this chapter just for women. Much of my experiences are also evident. Sometimes we get tired. Sometimes we are not able to express to our children or to anyone else the weariness on the beaten paths of life. That our feet are even able to take our bodies the unexplored distances in life is a testament to the psalmist's portrayal that we are "Fearfully and wonderfully made" (Psalm 139:14).

Langston Hughes spoke of a mother's conversation with her son.

> *Life for me ain't been no crystal stair.*
> *It's had tacks in it,*
> *And splinters,*
> *And boards torn up.*

It is amazing the distance and the path the feet must travel.... Women know all too well the paths they have taken in their lives. If as working women we could measure the distances we have traveled in the workplace alone, it is simply immeasurable.

The working mother's tired feet tarry day after day, doing the dance of her ancestors, whether it is hard labor or simply caring for her home—which can, at times, seem to turn into excessive slave labor and never-ending chores.

The reward is in knowing that you have contributed to the care and welfare of your family. We want our family to live in the comforts of well-kept shelter. We become a creative chief, preparing meals for disconcerting palates. It would appear that a woman was born with licenses for all worldly professions. She is a doctor, teacher, cook, makeshift mechanic, handywoman, gardener, chauffeur, and the list goes on. She performs her tasks with perfect certainty. Then, like a matriarch, she passes on her talents, and the cycle continues.

This sometimes-unappreciated woman takes any work to care for her family. Sometimes it is work that no longer leaves her hands soft and feminine but rough and dry, her feet tired and swollen. Yet she stands erect and proud. She has a family, and she must do whatever it takes to make things work, even ignoring her tired feet. Earning a day's wage is what she is after as she is determined to survive. She repeats this intermingled task with precision and dedication.

She rises up before her family; she is the Priest of that household, too. She has no time for illness, and sometimes pampering herself becomes second nature. Such was my life.

For twenty-six years, I held the position of single parent. I did nothing for myself, only for my family. I am now so socially awkward that being a spinster seems inevitable. This role swings on a pendulum between the married woman and the unmarried mother.

Something happened when the feminist movement took hold of the lives of women (I'm not blaming the movement—it was good). While women's rights were being fought for and accomplished, women at times encountered many additional hardships. More women were in the workplace, and more sons and daughters were left without the proper care from their mothers and their fathers.

These days, the roles have been reversed. Now women are tilling the ground and men are caring for the babies. More men are caring for their children at home and carrying them in baby pouches(admirable!), babysitting, cooking, house cleaning, laundering, and filing petitions for child support. There is nothing wrong with a man doing these duties. I am simply pointing out that life has gone to another extreme; roles have been reversed and accepted as the new norm.

It is my hope that women can examine their lives and realize that the Creator had a correct plan. Women should be and want to be treated like the Queens she is, while men want to be treated like the King they are and should be in the home.

Women and men still need helpmates. Ecclesiastes 4:9-11: "Two are better than one; because they have a good reward for their labor. For if they fall, the one will lift up his fellow; but woe to him that is alone when he falleth; for he hath not another to help him up. Again, I say if two lie together, then they have heat: but how can one be warm alone?" (KJV).

Ever notice what happens to a woman when she begins to do masculine duties? Her body begins to change; she starts to take on the contours of the male physique. She begins to lose her feminine sculpture and, in some cases, her mannerisms. This was not the Creator's plan.

Women are beautiful, as Maya Angelou wrote:

> *I say,*
> *It's in the reach of my arms,*
> *The span of my hips,*
> *The stride of my step,*
> *The curl of my lips...*
> *I say,*
> *It's the fire in my eyes,*
> *And flash of my teeth,*
> *The swing in my waist,*
> *And the joy in my feet....*

You can close your eyes and appreciate what a special creation you are to be a woman. I love being a woman. I would not have it any other way. I am feminine in every step, attitude, and part of my body. I just love me. I love the woman that God has created in me and the spiritual woman I am evolving to become.

Ladies…I believe life is good when you have someone to share it with. It is even better when you are single and love the Lord. If you are married, your Creator should be your first love. To all of us women, He is your someone, He is the lover of your soul.

In my vivid imagination, I love love. I believe there is nothing like the feeling of the masculine arms of your lover, your husband, your helpmate cradling your body, giving you the security that he has been ordained to demonstrate towards his love. Your feet should not be tired when there are two strong hands willing to massage your soles, allowing you to achieve the relaxation of sensual rest. (Smile, I just imagine that.) It is good thing to treated well and to want to be treated well. Some women have grown accustomed to settling for whatever they can get. At times, that is even abuse.

The women who have been blessed to have a Spirit-filled, God-fearing man appreciate him, and demonstrate their love by treating him with the respect, support, and assistance he needs to achieve his goals and aspirations, especially if you have already achieved them yourself. As he grows, grow with him. Seek to enhance yourself. I believe men are beautiful, especially when they are allowed to be the man God created them to be.

Finally, I believe that our Creator's arms are strong. He will never leave you disappointed or demand more than you are able to offer. He is our protector, our provider, and the lover of our souls. Psalms 91:4: "He shall cover thee with his feathers, and under his wings shall thou trust: His truth shall be thy shield and buckler" (KJV).

A verse in an old 19th century hymn by writer Horatius Bonar says:

> *I heard the voice of Jesus say,*
> *"Come unto Me, and rest;*
> *Lay down, thou weary one, lay down*
> *Thy head upon my breast."*
> *I came to Jesus as I was,*
> *Weary, and worn, and sad;*

I found in Him a resting place,
And he has made me glad.

Embrace Him, love Him, and He whose love is never ending will give you more love than you are able to hold. He allows your cup to overflow so that you can enjoy your overflow and never touch your cup. He is a God like no other God. He is constantly seeking ways to bless and provide for you. My sisters, you are loved, rest in Him. No more tired feet.

I was able to salvage some of my mother's poetic works.
I thought I would include at least one or two that I believed
were very special to her. They are deeply moving.
It is my final connection to a woman who spoke little, smiled a lot,
and had few friends.

ଙ

HOPE

Do you have hands that I can touch for I
desire to hold them very much?

I lie awake at nights with thoughts just to name a few

Just wondering what it would be like lying next to you

Where do you abide? Hope, please give me a clue

For without you, my future looks dauntingly blue

Do you have eyes? Can't you see my sadness?

If only I could see you, I know they'll change to gladness

Oh, hope, tell me where you are

From where I sit you seem so far, I long to be
near you. I long to hear your voice

Why do you hide yourself from me? And leave me without a choice?

Or should I look much closer and not where angels fear to tread

For some far distance I really dread

Maybe you are just around the corner, just a little up ahead

Or are you right next to me and I am
looking at something else instead?

Hope, please don't elude me now

I can't give up on you. So please, won't you tell me? Where to find you

I must continue to look for you even though I'm weary

For life without you would be very dreary

When I find you, hope, we will plan for our future together

And when our lives intertwine, things will be much better

Dear hope, I long to feel your touch and tell
you my needs are such and such

If you are near me, show me a sign, and if
you have hands, clasp them in mine

O hope, I await your gentle touch

For I desire you very much

Mrs. Jeanette V. Nurse (My Mother)

Chapter 6

KNOWING YOUR WORTH

There is a delightful little parable, told by philosopher Soren Kierkegaard. One night, a group of thieves did a different kind of stealing. They broke into a jewelry store, not to steal but to switch the prices on every item in the store. The next day, no one could tell what was valuable and what was cheap. No one knew what they were purchasing. Some who thought they were purchasing valuable gems were purchasing costume jewelry. Those who could not afford the higher-priced items were leaving the store with highly valued treasures.

This little parable reminds me of Matthew 6:19-21: "Do not store up for yourselves treasures on earth, where moth and vermin destroy, and where thieves break in and steal. But store up for yourselves treasures in heaven, where moth and vermin do not destroy and where thieves do not break in and steal. For where your treasure is, there your heart will be also" (NIV).

I make this correlation with the value of our lives and knowing our own worth. How can one know what is valuable? We need a spiritual connection or a deeper understanding of what is worthy and valuable in our lives.

I believe the person with discerning spiritual character, who is spiritually directed, is able to search the scriptures and find the treasures of the anointing words that God has placed within.

I believe at times we lack the proper discernment in our search for a mate and in our search for the joy of life. Many who embark on the search for a mate may first want to feast on the words of Proverbs 3:5-6: "Trust in the Lord with all thine heart; and lean not unto thine own understanding, in all thine ways acknowledge him, and he shall direct thy path" (KJV).

God knows the needs of His children. According to Proverbs 18:22: "Who so findeth a wife, findeth a good thing and obtain favor from the Lord" (KJV). Favor is extended to that man whom the Spirit has directed to his mate. The bible says the Lord placed Adam asleep while he created for him a helpmate. Every animal was paired accordingly, but there was no pair for Adam.

It was not she who found and obtained favor. Adam was the only man whom God assisted to find a mate. Lest God should be blamed not of manipulating man's choice, man must now find his own wife. God may assist with putting her on his path, but he needs to now spiritually discern God's Spirit within her. He himself should also possess the character of God.

There are those who have an eye for the valuable and know the worth of specific gems. They can discern between a ruby, a diamond, and pure jade. For me, I like clothes. I can tell top-quality linen, a linen-rayon mix, wool, Jaccard, and on and on. I can see the beauty in the cloth and how it makes the body look elegant. I love stylish clothing. I believe a woman should look classy.

I enjoy Afrocentric art and Afrocentric clothing. I also enjoy fine art, porcelain, paintings, old artistic pictures, especially black and white prints with fine lines. I enjoy the beautiful satire of poetry, I love the elegance of old brooches. And my list goes on.

I love to comprehend the worth and beauty of my choices. Even in simplicity, I enjoy the beauty of an item. Some of these things bring joy to me. I go to an innate place of beauty, worth, and value.

I enjoy finding treasures at thrift stores. I am attracted to anything vintage or antique. I also enjoy flea markets for the haggle of the bargain. So fun. I find joy in colors—colors in my clothes and colors in my home. Decorating brings me joy, especially with artistic pieces.

I do my best to surround myself with beautiful objects. That is my eye and the creative side of me. I enjoy a good sense of humor, which is an art in itself.

I love to laugh, and laughter has been a comfort throughout my life. I know how to laugh at myself and with myself. Saying something humorous is my go-to place. I enjoy attending church and planning church programs. Church has been my primary recreation and source of spiritual growth. I seldom go out, and dating has become obsolete. Sounds like a boring life, but I love it.

Imagine Adam's observation of Eve: He was able to see her for what she was—a gem. There was no other like her. She was original and coveted. She was accepted at first glance. She was a treasure. She was valuable and worthy. Adam saw in her a fine discovery. He was awestruck at the treasure that was before him.

I believe we all have to tap into hearing the Spirit speak. He speaks in clear tones. In your meditation, He directs and orders our steps. He protects and covers. He admonishes and prepares. He is the Holy Spirit, He dwells within.

I refer you to the above-mentioned tale to encourage you not to allow anyone to steal your value. There is a wonderful bible verse I have come to appreciate as my inspiration in Matthew 7:6: "Do not give what is holy to dogs, and do not throw pearls before swine, lest they trample them under their feet, and turn and tear you to pieces" (NKJV).

I look at life very differently now, given the multiple ordeals that I have endured. I have come to appreciate and realize my worth. I identify with the pearl and the diamond. In my mind, I am a pearl surrounded by diamonds. A pearl because of the discomforts, pains, and disappointments I have had to endure. It has not been easy to recognize my worth. It was as if I gave away that which was of most value in exchange for things and people in my life that were costume jewelry. Because I lacked my own discernment, I became a target for deception.

But while the pearl glows, the diamond glistens. I now see myself as a pearl surrounded by diamonds because of the pressures I have had to endure to achieve my glow. My beauty shines through in the smoothness of the precious pearl, while the diamond shines through with the indwelling of the Holy Spirit in my life. When light is illumined in me, I feel the positive transformation of the spiritual indwelling. I am truly grateful. I realize that the struggles I endured and am enduring were and are only to enhance, to bring to the surface the beauty of me and the glow of my spirit.

William Shakespeare wrote these words in *Othello*:

> *Good name in man and woman, dear my lord,*
> *Is the immediate jewel of their souls:*
> *Who steals my purse steals trash; 'tis something, nothing;*
> *'twas mine, 'tis his, and has been slaves to thousands;*
> *But he that filches from me my good name*
> *Robs me of that which not enriches him,*
> *And makes me poor indeed.*

So beautiful. To be robbed of your name, that which brings dignity of identifying specifically who you are, is to be robbed of your worth, if you will.

Sometimes people tell me I resemble someone they have either seen in another country or someone in general. I always respond sarcastically, "No one looks like me. I am an original." Now that I know and understand my worth. A counterfeit may have the appearance of an original, yet it is worth nothing and has no value. A person who may resemble me should be proud of their own appearance; they are non-comparative to this one-of-a-kind pearl that is in me. I am truly blessed. In my Heavenly Father's eyes, I glow because His Spirit is upon me.

In the play *The Merchant of Venice*, Shakespeare wrote:

> *[The quality of mercy] is twice blessed;*
> *It blesseth him that gives, and him that takes;*
> *'T is mightiest in the mightiest; it becomes*
> *The throned monarch, better than his crown.*

Mercy has been extended to me in more ways than I can testify.

I write because I must leave a legacy for my children's children. Their name is important. They come from a lineage of strength, of Kings and Queens, of love and of praise and of worship to a God who saves, who provides, and who is coming again.

I love my name; it was given to me by my grandmother. She gave me the name of two Queens, both biblical. She saw in me a Queen. My first name, Esther, means star, which I love. That was the shine my mother also saw in me. It is my glow. I can also be referred to as Hadassah. My middle name, Cleopatra, means glory of her father. Imagine that! I was born a star with the glory of my father. I like to believe that I have the glow of my Heavenly Father. I resemble Him and His character is in me.

The glow that I possess must be obvious and real because even the woman who painted my portrait said she saw a glow. She painted the portrait as she observed the sun on my face and the moon at my back. I pray that I can transcend whatever others see in me, to bring healing to anyone in my presence.

What a wise woman my grandmother was to be led by the Spirit. My grandmother knew my worth. It is I who did not know my worth. It is I who switched roles, like the Mark Twain story of the Prince and the Pauper. This tale has been handed down through the generations, each father telling his sons. Just as I must share with my children and their children. According to the preface of the book *The Prince and the Pauper*, it is not particularly known whether this tale was true or not; however, it drives home a point.

In our lives, we are always fascinated by the unknown and the unexplored. We are always seeking to find that which will bring us happiness, not realizing it is joy that we truly need. Joy comes from God.

In our inquisitiveness, we find a world full of trouble. Stepping out of the protective embrace, we find an unfamiliar world. Our next recourse is to then call upon the Lord. "Lord, save me, I am in great distress, I have not found that which I sought in the world. Please save me." Often that follows with the phrase, "If you help me, Lord, I will never do this or that again." We often make promises to God at the moment of our situation but soon forget. Sometimes we even stretch our truth to say, "Lord, I will do this in your honor, I will be the best child you created." Isn't it wonderful that we have a God who is acquainted with all of our ways?

The bible says God "winks at our ignorance..." Acts 17:30, KJV). I have been in many precarious situations, and I must confess I did not receive the punishment I deserve, although I do have some scars to remind me. The scars will never go away, but God's Word will continue to stand the test of time.

Another impacting quote that has inspired me comes from the 19th century English preacher, Matthew Henry. One day he was robbed. In the evening, he wrote in his diary:

> *I was robbed today and I thank thee first because I was never robbed before; second, because although they took my purse, they did not take my life; third, because although they took my all, it was not much; and fourth, because it was I who was robbed and not I who robbed.*

I am so impressed with this quote because this man, in his evaluation of his circumstance, was able to acknowledge his unfortunate encounter, be thankful for his life, and understand that the treasure was not in what he had or in its quantity. This man admired and elevated the pride of his character. The treasure was within.

Isn't it wonderful to have such self-worth that, though you may have endured all kind of crucibles, your spirit can remain strong, steadfast, and hopeful when you realize the worth and worthiness of your character and the spiritual being that you have been created to be.

My life is a life of great gratitude. I have come to a place where I am now able to see the value of me, the value of the person who was the prize, but who switched my place of worth to explore a pauper's life. A jewel with a crown, casting my pearls before swine. A Queen seeking to regain her God-given status. I am a woman, glad to be called a child of the King, and therefore, I must comport myself as such. I am the King's daughter. My greatest wish for my children and my children's children is that they know their worth and embrace their challenges in life.

My spirit is at peace. I look to the Holy Spirit for his infilling. I have been humbled. I have been spared for such a time as this. Gratefulness is my utmost gratitude.

I LOOKED FOR SOMEONE

This morning I looked for someone to pray
with me because I was all alone

I called a few persons on a dial tone

But no one picked up the phone

Then I called to Jesus and said, Lord, please pray for me

For I'm in need of Your strength

Please let me lean on Thee

Later the phone rang and I wondered who could it be

Someone called to pray and encourage me

They said tell it all to your older brother and make your stand

Dear Jesus, You're my special someone who cares and understands

For you know the hairs on my head and I'm in the palm of your hand

My heart was full and I told it all to Jesus, as by the altar he stood

I said, Jesus, please help me if only you would

He looked at me and I heard him say, "My
child, I'll do all that I could."

Now when I need someone, I'll follow this prayer trend

I'll dial his number and he'll answer me,
because He is always there, and

He is my friend

Mrs. Jeanette V. Nurse

Chapter 7

REJECTED NO MORE

In my life, I have known and loved three men. I call it my stolen innocence years. There was a fourth puppy love, infatuation; I was only a child at the time of our meeting. I was eleven years old; he was much older. Without discussing much about him, I will only discuss the three that I came to know during my teenage to adult years.

I was rejected by all three of these "loves of my life." I suppose if I sought comfort in my past, the fourth was the only one who truly loved me. He was the man for whom I never returned to my homeland to marry. At the time I left my country, I was a teenager, but the promise was that I would return. He waited for two to three years. That was a man dedicated. The rest is history. He eventually found someone.

Let's talk about my rejected loves. None of these men saw me as a woman to be honored, a woman to be treasured, a woman who was the child of a King. They each thought somebody else's daughter was more honorable. "I was somebody's daughter too." Most of all, I belonged to the King. Now that I think about it, this was part of my pauper's life.

A

Of the three, I loved the third and last the most. He stole my heart. I met him at a time when I felt I was truly ready to begin another relationship. Reflecting on this, there was so much I did not know and

I was not ready at all. I had felt I was sufficiently healed from my second very traumatic relationship. I felt more mature and with clearer sight. After not being involved with anyone for more than eleven years, I was now in my forties and ready to move forward.

I was so immersed in loving this man that the realization of being in a mental relationship all by myself was a distant thought. It was the start of a roller-coaster ride, without protection. I became blinded to reasonable advice. My mental readiness for love and romance presented an obstacle to visual insight. I was excited that a man seemingly had any interest in me.

I suppose somehow this man could observe the greenness of my persona, yet I was ripe for his picking. I expected bliss. I wanted bliss, so I created my own fantasies. My expectation became my disappointment. Many days, I wondered: What was my problem? Not his problem. It was I who caused him not to want me or to show me the good time I had expected. I had naively opened myself to a person for whom I was no match. There were walls in every direction I turned with this man. I was trapped before I had any awareness.

Nothing I did pleased him; nevertheless, I continued on my quest to please him at all costs, even my own unhappiness. I never divulged to him my unhappiness because I feared losing him. I never received any real happiness or joy. I had no time together, no gifts, no flowers, no romantic letters or cards, no romantic conversations, no going out, no assistance.... I kept loving him, holding on to hope for what appeared to be dear life.

I kept the hope in my wait; if I waited long enough, I would be privy to better days. I couldn't imagine it would be such a difficult challenge. It should not have been a challenge, but this was the atmosphere of my mental trap.

This experience allowed me to evaluate it with deep thought; God, I thought, how did I find myself in this place? "It is not supposed to be this way." Looking at other relationships, what was wrong with the one I wanted? I had not been involved with anyone; why was I being dealt this hand?

I began to slowly realize, as the Spirit brought back to my memory, that when God does anything for His children, it is well done. He says, "For I know the thoughts that I think towards you, saith the Lord, thoughts of peace and not of evil, to give you an expected end" (Jeremiah 29:11, KJV).

I was working so hard that at times I felt out of breath. I was always racing towards a mirage. Why was it so difficult for me to find love or one to love me? Many times, I tried to escape; somehow, he would anticipate my intent and would lure me back with what seemed to be the sweetest conversation or some form of humor.

At times, I wanted to believe his thoughts; this one was so easy to manipulate. It took much prayer and meditation to finally hear and listen to the Spirit speaking. I am not saying it was easy for me. It was my mental affections, and it seemed surgery was needed on my mind. This surgery could not be performed with ordinary hands. I would have to receive a severe severing of myself from my mental affections.

Gone are the days when an old mother of the church could recommend that a young lady choose a man from the church—or rather that a man from the church would choose her. Something has happened to our men. They no longer desire to have a good church girl—well, maybe some.

I don't want to say I was used; rather, this man chose not to honor me. In turn, at the time, I did not honor myself. I could not see my worth. My worth was wrapped up in being accepted by others, particularly a man who did not love me or could not love.

In the last conversation I had with my mother while on her dying bed, I expressed my unhappiness with my involvement. She turned her head in my direction and looked at me. With some hesitation, but with clarity, she said, "That man never liked you.... It is you who does not want to let go of him." Then she added, after a pause, "Let the man go." I remembered just staring at her, feeling ashamed and numb. It would be the last time my mother and I would have a meaningful conversation.

What was it about this third man? I loved his voice, I loved his physique, I loved his quiet spirit, I loved our conversations—more so his conversations. This was how he kept me at bay. It was his topic, and he decided when he wanted the conversation to end. Somehow, I had some contentment with this one-sided arrangement because I just wanted him to talk to me. It was my feeling that he was definitely the man. I just knew he was my soulmate. I even called him my best friend. I was involved in an unholy soul tie that would trap me for five years of my life. Feelings are misguided. Feelings change, feelings are sporadic and unpredictable. Trusting your feelings is a gamble. This was a lesson I learned harshly.

He wanted my companionship only at times to satisfy his own gratifications. When he wanted to talk, I deprived myself to listen to only what he wanted to talk about. One day he told me, "I want to talk about what I want." I entertained this behavior because I just had to have him in my life.

He played the game well. Even when one day he said, nonchalantly, "I hope your parents will not hate me because I will never marry their daughter." Somehow, it was as if I was hypnotized. Nothing was resonating. I could not even hear rejection. I just wanted to love him and he to love me back.

He spent very little time with me. In the five years I knew him, he never slept at my home, he never spent a weekend with me. We never spent a holiday together. I could count the few times we went out. Probably about five times might be a stretch. I was waiting, waiting... I was going to be the perfect little overachiever and wait, not pushing any buttons. He was going to be mine and I was going to be his. He was always fixing himself, so again I had to wait. My investment, no returns.

I would later find out that this man did not belong to me. He always had another. He took what he needed from me, then he returned to her. She was his prize. I was the side dish; he could take it or leave it. These are the events that happen when you lead a pauper's life.

I would continue in my stupor for more years than I now care to remember. I was a woman chasing love and I had the energy for it. I wanted to become entangled with what some women are now seeking to get out of; I was racing to get in.

I felt like the woman at the well. In Jesus's conversation with her, he was able to reveal: "for you have had five husbands, and the one whom you now have is not your husband, in that you spoke truly" (John 4:16-18, NKJ). In many ways, I was that woman. I was met by my Savior but still had questions. I did not realize the depth of my condition. I was wading in filth but adapted to the stench as if it was the norm.

I refused to dismiss the thought that I could not have the fairytale romance and the happily-ever-after. After all, it was God who created woman for man and even placed her on his path. It was God who said, "It is not good for man to be alone…" (Genesis 2:18, NKJ).

I was a woman, I was created by Him. Surely there must be an Adam for me. I felt I was beautiful. Perhaps I did not have Eve's body, but I still looked good. Surely I was bone of bone from some man's body. What was the problem?

It is interesting that my blindness was so deep, I refused to see the narcissist in the treatment I received. I was certain it was love. He played a game of cat and mouse that I now clearly realize he alone enjoyed. I was the mouse, and the cat enjoyed the power he had over the game. To coin a phrase, "I was a glutton for punishment." All in the name of chasing love.

I soon realized through spiritual intervention that love was with me all along. Love stood by my side, love beckoned me to His embrace. Love covered me at night in my exhaustion, love longed to fill me. That love was divine, that love was the Holy Spirit. How else was I going to glow? My glow comes from the Spirit within.

I have ended all notions that life would be different for me with this man. He always belonged to another. I could no longer hurt myself. It is not God's plan. I know now that if it is God's will, it is in His time and it will be on time.

I was an overachiever. The reason for my overachievement, I believe, grew out of my parents' disappointment with my first pregnancy. Even the pregnancies of my last two children were disappointments to them. I tried my best to make up for my indiscretions.

I completed college in four years, not the five that I was expected to, since I was behind. I worked two jobs while trying to raise my baby boy as a young mother. My son was nine months old when I returned to school. I took intersession classes, I took summer classes, all I could do was just to prove I was not a disappointment.

To everything I did, I gave one hundred and ten percent. If I gave someone a gift, it had to be the best gift. I would spend endless hours analyzing a person's character, and anything I did for anyone was because I had gotten so close to their spirit that satisfaction was always a success.

This has been the spirit of my entire life. I give of myself wholeheartedly to relationships, to projects, to my church, to work. I remember one of my supervisors and my coworkers crying when I left one of my jobs. My church hated to see me leave when I relocated. They threw me the biggest going-away send-off; these people would miss the gem they came to know.

I was and still am a gem to all who come in contact with me. While my internal struggles were real, I refused to allow anyone to observe that I lacked anything, that I was hurt, that I was lonely, that I needed a true friend.

The one gift I wanted…eluded me to this day. I chased that gift as if it had been a must-have trophy. The more I chased it, the more it eluded me. I was driven by my overachieving attitude. I wanted to be loved by a man. God's Agape love was and is free. I chose to pay for mine and still lost.

B

Love number two…there is much to say about this individual. I must shorten this experience for fear that I will lose my forgiveness. He was the man I met upon completing college; I was twenty-three, he was thirty-six. There I go again with these older men.

It was my naïve thought that the process was as follows: complete your education, get happily married, purchase a home (the one with the white picket fence), have children, avoid disputes in the home, travel the world, and grow old together. What an imagination.

I remember meeting this man when I began my first real job. I was going to change the world. There was nothing this twenty-three-year-old could not accomplish. I had already had a child, and now I was working a good job, getting benefits, and earning my desired salary at the time—$23,000 a year...wow, I just dated myself! I was on top of the world. I just had to find a partner to share my enthusiasm. I did not really know the Lord as I do now. I had left the church during the time I met this man.

I was in love. I chased this man with romantic gifts and romantic cards (never received any gifts from him). I was fascinated with him. He was exotic, a foreigner, and my interest was even more piqued. I was going to get him; I became the hunter (mistake number one). I got him all right...him and the five or so other women he managed. Little did I know this would be another ride of my life. Always on fast rides. Young and inexperienced with the world. Remember, I was going to change the world. Wrong!

I loved this man. I gave him money, I cooked food for him purchased with my own money. In the meantime, I yearned to spend time with him. He stayed at his home and I at mine. Another of my mental relationships. I eventually became pregnant again at age twenty-five. I was going to do anything to have this man, including bear children. In my young mind, a child would draw us closer. I became a Leah (Genesis 29:30, KJV), never seeming to gain the affections of those I loved yet producing children for them. Nevertheless, God still watched and cared for me.

When I became pregnant with our first child, my vulnerability was in a critical state. My finances were low, and I was fearful of having to raise two children on my own. I recalled begging to move in with him. He asked, "What is going to become of my privacy?" He then added, "I cannot marry you because you are not a virgin."

I would have to raise these children by myself. I was now a single parent of two. I continued to love this man, regardless of his callousness towards me; I was sure he was going to love me eventually. I became pregnant with a second child. I was now a single parent to three. My situation was becoming a nightmare. How was I going to raise three children on one job, no support, and an emotionally abusive relationship?

It was at this point that I returned to the church. God was calling me. Daily, I would pass a specific church on my way to and from work. It was as if the church was speaking to me, especially on my way home from work. At times, I would have to restrain myself from looking at the building. I found myself hiding behind the sides of the bus. This went on for some time.

I was having a private tug-of-war with the Holy Spirit. I'm so glad He favored me. God wanted to save me and I wanted to be saved, but I was afraid. How was I going to return to the church? After leaving the first time, I ended up with a bad relationship and two unplanned children.

One Sabbath morning, I found myself in that very church building. My life would not be the same. I dressed my children in whatever they had. My daughter was two years old at the time. I was so frightened that my legs trembled. I held my children so close to me, it was as if we were welded together. My children were also feeling my fears. That day passed.

Returning to the church was not all smooth sailing. I encountered some difficulties that were strategically designed by the enemy to push me back out of the church. Some people tried to silence me because I was not yet a member. There were those who were offended by the often-loud wails of a two-year-old unaccustomed to being in a church. Not to mention those who held seats for their friends. Then, there were those who approached me for unexpected favors. The father of my children challenged my attending church with his children. The struggle was at times a place of much discouragement. I would have to be the priest of my home, and I would have to save my children.

I was determined to persevere. I re-baptized and joined the church. My children were eventually baptized. I would eventually hold multiple leadership positions. I was instrumental in starting specific programs in the church. At times, I held two major positions. I even discovered I could sing. My first song was "Like a Woman at the Well." I perfected that song. I must say that I have never left, and I am still in the church. To God be the glory.

My relationship with this man ended very volatilely. My children were now scattered. My life would change forever, all because of my poor choices in relationships.

Through it all, my life has been a blessing. When you begin to act as though your life is a blessing, you will soon realize it begins to feel like one. It is now my desire to be a blessing to anyone who may need my help. I have gone through some not-so-proud situations.

My choices were not Spirit-led. God worked with my choices; I would not escape the scars my choices would bring. Nevertheless, I am still here, saved by His Grace and Glowing.

C

The final relationship I will describe was my first. I met him when I was sixteen, he was twenty-two. He was the cutest thing. He had a head full of hair, which he kept in the weirdest style. He was a quiet man who spoke as if he was shy. He was always leaning his head to the side and never really made eye contact. He was just lovable. Everybody loved him. He was kind and would do anything for anyone. He was good with his hands and anything electronic. Conveniently, we lived in the same building, he on the first floor and I on the fifth.

We had easy access to each other. After school, I couldn't wait to return home. I was exploring all that life had to offer, even learning how to kiss among the explorations. It would be good gleeful conversations for my best friend and me. I was excited. I was in love. I want to believe he loved me too. He was also a foreigner, although our cultures were not of great distinctions. We could understand each other. It was unfortunate that his parents were not having me. They preferred his other girl; she was directly from his culture and his country.

I was seventeen when we became intimate. One month after my eighteenth birthday, I was a mother. I was oblivious to life and what path I would tread. My life seemed to come to a crushing halt and an eye-opening experience.

I was a mother with no real knowledge of what was happening. I did not even know that babies moved in the stomach. I would often feel the movement and become afraid. I never told anyone. I was too afraid to talk to my mother. At the time, she was also pregnant with my brother. Yes, you guessed it: My son has an uncle who is two months younger than he is.

What a situation I was in! During my time in high school, I was part of an elite group who were the smartest in the same class. We ate together and we attended every subject together. College-bound, it was evident that we all would become the best of our career choices. I was accepted to college and expected to enter the same month when my baby was born.

Everything became an unpredictable change. Graduating from high school while six months pregnant, jobless, and living at home with parents with whom I did not have much of a relationship. I spent much of my pregnancy in my own room, only venturing out for some food after everyone had turned in. I was alone and ashamed. I did not want my parents to see my growing stomach. The summer was hot; sometimes I just wanted to strip and walk around the house, but I could not. I stayed in my hot room. I shopped for baby items with the little money I received from public assistance.

This man who was the love of my life was of no help. He lived with his mother. She informed me that the only help she could give me was if I needed food. I was now a casualty. He no longer desired my body. He had another.

Imagine when I found out he had another child, born a few months before mine. What is it with me and these men who belonged to others? I was a naïve youth with no real directives. I did not have the love of a father, and it seemed like my mother and I were like sisters. After all, she was only sixteen years older than I.

I really don't recall how our relationship ended. I eventually entered college, and he pursued other paths. He eventually had to return to reside in his country.

My single-parent life began at eighteen years. I was a single parent for twenty-six years. You already know the rest of the story. God always has a plan for His children's lives. He wants to give us good gifts, the greatest of which is the Holy Spirit. According to Matthew 7:11, "If ye then, being evil, know how to give good gifts unto your children, how much more shall your father which… is in heaven give good things to those who ask him!" (KJV).

I want to attribute my disappointments and my poor choices to what may have stemmed from a much deeper place. I believe it began with my two fathers. I had a biological father and a stepfather. My biological father rejected me because he wanted a male child. My stepfather, although a man with many children, did not know himself; therefore, how could he be a true father to me? I must say that he did adopt me and I carry his last name, but that is a story for another book. He was the only father I knew for many years. Now I embrace my Heavenly Father, who is all that is true to me.

After all that I have experienced, I must now embrace Christ and my Heavenly Father alone. My Salvation has become very personal to me. I must relearn to trust again. At this point, it is a distant thought, yet I am exploring my faith and my pertinence diligently. I have given so much of myself that I cannot afford to lose anymore of me.

Someone once said to me that every time someone uses you, they take a piece of you. With enough of these pieces removed, you are left fractured and almost incapacitated. The key aspect of broken relationships is that the person involved often does not realize pieces of their persona are being slowly stolen. It is much like the frog in water as the temperature slowly rises. The frog is soon cooked before he realizes it is time to jump out.

I smile to myself when I think that I was such a romantic at heart, with no one to romance or be romanced by. But wait, that is not true. I have a Heavenly Father. He romances me daily with His love, for He is love.

It is unfortunate that it took until I entered my fifties to realize finally that love was always with me, and that which I chased was a fleeting mirage of a joy that cannot be realized without my Heavenly Father's blessings and according to his time. He who began a good work in me will be faithful to complete it.

In all, I must say that learning to love yourself will be the essence of my transformation and a step into a new beginning of life. I believe

I lacked self-love; therefore, it became easy to become trapped with a failure to recognize what true love is.

I now know that in order to learn how to love, I must first ask my Creator to be my teacher. He who encompasses love must now teach me to recognize love within myself.

Chapter 8

SACRED LOVE

As long as I can remember, I have romanticized marriage and finding the love of my life. As a young woman every year until I reached my fifties, I planned my wedding. I just knew that it was going to happen for me. I endured years of abuse by the men in my life because I wanted so much to be loved.

I forgot the originator of love—He who says, "Love is patient, Love is kind and is not puffed up" (1Cor 13, KJV). He who endured the Cross because of love. Love does not hurt. I wanted to be loved. I have never met a man who loved me. That includes the fathers who were in my life.

Many of my years were spent with much heartbreak. The last relationship I endured ended with taunts of "You wanted marriage, but I just want a friend." This was after at least five years of knowing this individual. I was discarded and rejected again.

That man found his joy at my expense. I was deprived because I was just not the woman in whom he had any interest to share that experience. Perhaps there was some other reason I am unable to explain. Unfortunately for that man, good gifts of worth can only be recognized by he who is worthy of the gift. So, let me talk a little about my view of marriage.

Marriage…a subject that seems to maneuver its way into the minds of every young, middle-aged, or elderly, healthy-minded, single woman or man. Of course, it is only for those with a desire to be joined in holy matrimony. This group excludes those I term "children," such as immature teenagers. Simply put, marriage is not for children.

It appears that an innate clock switches on, inviting conversations of exclusive relationship bonding. But do those who entertain such thoughts comprehend the magnitude of their desires? Do they understand the sacredness of this wonderful gift, given to us by our Creator? Do they comprehend that those vows are not recitations? That sharing their life with another human being is a special act, ordained by spiritual intervention.

Marriage to me is a connection made in heaven and sanctioned by the Creator. So, when the vows "To love, cherish, honor, obey in sickness, in health, until death are you to be separated" are desecrated and violated, it can be described as a cruel demise and demolition of the spirit of the person being hurt.

This disconnection makes sounds that resonate through the heart like electrical waves, causing the body to vibrate like a never-ending shock. It is at this time that the sacredness of love should be realized, although I do believe only discerning, spirit-filled hearts who embrace this transition with Godly obedience will enjoy the bliss that should come with marriage, the way God ordained it to be. There are ups and downs in any relationship, and anyone embarking on this union must enter with that understanding. There will not always be mountain-top experiences.

When the Creator bonds two "whole" people (persons who know themselves first, both physically and spiritually) together to form a oneness, it is a joining that is sacred. If you are considering someone as your other half or life partner to make you whole, then you have not realized your own spiritual wholeness.

You have not realized or have a concept of how sacred you are to be a "whole" spiritually filled person. You need to be proud of your accomplishments; you must have an idea of where you are going and a clear view of your future before you join with another.

In what I would call my gullible years, I recall saying to a man, "You are my other half." I did not realize my completeness in the person I was created to be. I did not realize my completeness in the Spirit that was within me. I sought love and completeness in the arms of strangers, men who did not know me or did not care to know the complete woman.

I was not a sacred love to them. Seeking completeness in the arms of human beings is a trap into which lonely men and women allow themselves to fall. They have convinced themselves that because they are single, the spirit of loneliness is allowed to take up permanent lodging.

My advice is to kill that lonely spirit, plug up its holes, and allow no room for its enticement or entertainment. Let the lover of your soul engulf you in those moments when you feel you are alone. Sacred love will mystify you like glorious rays of light that elevate you in weightless motions, drawing you to its luminous presence. God's love is sacred.

Why is it that women, and some men, feel the need to seek completeness from others when the Creator clearly said, "Being confident of this very thing, that He which had begun a good work in you, will perform it until the day of Jesus Christ" (Philippians 1:6, KJV). God will give you your completeness.

I am what you would term an "incurable romantic," yet I also consider myself cynical. I love the romanticism of marriage, falling in love, intimacy, family, and the fantasy of a fairytale wedding, but the cynicism comes when I hear the pains and struggles of couples, when I hear of divorce and abuses. During these times, I think marriage is only a fantasy or a means by which men and women torture themselves into believing they have now embraced happiness.

There is a Percy Sledge song that says, "When a man loves a woman, she can do no wrong, turn his back on his best friend if he puts her down." These songs are sometimes the luring fantasy that lulls a woman or a man into a hypnotic stupor, believing this is the one who completes her or him. Therefore, they will sometimes even put their family and friends to the side to enjoy this newfound happiness.

A man or a woman clings to the fantasy that a daily walk is ordered by only soft steps upon petals. Sometimes, it takes but a few hours for those petals to feel like the "little shop of horrors." That is when someone's persona begins to take on its true character. My cynical view is not always the case since many relationships have stood the test of time.

It is said, "And Adam knew Eve his wife and she conceived and bore a son" (Genesis, KJV). This was the sacred love union that produced fruitful gain. Some unions have not produced a child but have remained happy. When trust is put in God, He is the binding cord for a sacred union.

When I think of sacred love, I think of Adam looking at his wife in unexplained awe, absorbing the essence of her countenance which invited his response: "And Adam said, this is now bone of my bones, and flesh of my flesh: she shall be called woman, because she was taken out of man" (Genesis 2:3, KJV).

Imagine being so highly regarded that when your spouse looks at you, he or she observes that your union is spiritually blessed. You are both whole people building on God and each other. Can you feel the sacredness of love? Can you comprehend the depth of love that flows from our Creator's imagination?

I love love. And I have tremendous respect for those who have achieved a relationship that is built on the love of God, the love for each other, and the deep comprehension that there is a sacred order to the union—a union created for man and woman.

By now, you have realized that I have not been privileged with the union of marriage. Perhaps this will someday be God's will. To those who have gracefully received the gift of marriage, I say treasure what you have and let the Creator be the revealer to order your steps, as you contemplate what sacred love means to you. We are living in a time when it is becoming increasingly difficult to truly grasp the sacredness of marriage and love as our Creator has ordained.

My sisters and brothers, someone once told me, "If it is the Lord's will that I remain a veteran of Challenges," and "Our lives without trouble are a dead life; but in spite of it all we can live our best life." I pray that these experiences will entice you to take a fresh look at your life and the closeness with which you are walking with the Creator.

This is the last legacy that I have of my mother.

In her own words, she penned the following words to me on my thirty-ninth birthday.

Love is restored in my heart. The woman I really did know as I should have.

May she rest in peace.

☙

From Mother to Daughter

YOU ARE

Was it only yesterday I saw you for the first time?

I smiled and said you are mine

My, oh my, you grew up pretty fine

And yes, you are always on my mind

Even now that you are thirty and nine

I am proud of you, for you are like a bright sunshine

Yes, you are; you are born to shine

And that is why I love you

Because you are!

From Mommy

Let's just say the years have flown by since I was thirty-nine years old. I have attempted to write this book numerous times. Somehow the time never seemed to be right, the words never seemed to flow. I often thought to myself: With all the books in the world, who would want to read mine? Of course, I spoke from my wilderness place. I am coming out now. Psalms 19:4-6 says, "In them hath he set a tabernacle for the sun, which is as a bridegroom coming out of his chamber, and rejoiceth as a strong man to run a race. His going forth is from the end of the heaven, and his circuit unto the ends of it: and there is nothing hid from the heath thereof" (KJV). The Artist got it right. My Glow is heavenly.

The time has finally come for me to shine. It is my hope that this book will be an accomplishment that will be a blessing to many who desire to see the miracle of the Holy Spirit working in their lives.

Thank you, Mommy, for seeing the light in me. Thank you for the life you birthed in me. Thank you for the moments we spent together.

I hated seeing my mother in a nursing home. I hated going to visit her there because it was a nursing home. It seemed like a last-stop place. What I wouldn't give now to just have a moment, a word from her lips.

This poem was the best gift I ever received from anyone. My Mom is gone now. I am her legacy.

FREEDOM

Finally, the freedom to love

The freedom to cry

The freedom to explore self, life, wants and desires

Like the flow of water as it finds its way around its obstacle course

Flow, freedom, flow…

The trees and leaves sway to their own music of freedom

Freedom to express the desires of life

Like a flag, embracing the free flow of the wind

The mountains sing, the eagles glide, they understand the how

Freedom knows no height

It grows with a light that engulfs the darkness of life

Freedom grows with every moment of awakened desires

It fights the battle of the enslaved

Transforms the mind, unlocks the captured spirit

Tapping into the creative talents, utilizing the entire capacity of the brain

Freedom lives within the crevices of every blood vessel, muscle, cartilage, and sinew

It is wrapped up in our being

Freedom flows like a dream

It is colorful, creates its own images, completing a work of art

Freedom is beautiful, it is everlasting

It holds no captives

It soars, creates, invites, exhales, inhales.

Free, free, Freedom…

Find it…hold on to it…it is yours

Freedom awaits your embrace

Finally, finally, freedom to love, to create, to explore, to climb

To dismantle obstacles

Finally, freedom!!

Esther C. Nurse

MY PRAYER

I pray as I walk with Jesus; His spirit continues to overflow. His light illuminates my spirit. As I look to You, Lord, I pray that You will give me the strength to keep my eyes steady on You, Lord.

In spite of all of my faults, shameful acts, unnecessary falls, my failures to listen to Your still small voice, and my many scars, I am grateful that You spared my life.

I am grateful for life, for Your love, and for my testimony. Thank You, Lord, for my bruises and all of my pains. Now I walk with a God who is acquainted with all that ails me, with all of my indiscretions, my anger and my needs. I no longer have to be ashamed. I walk with a God who has set me free. A God who has broken my chains. A God who died for my sins. A God who endured pain and bruising that I might live.

I now look to a God who has supplied all my needs and heals my ailments. A God who loves so deeply He never leaves my side. A God who does not sleep, always working for my good. Oh, that we should trust You, Lord. That the trying of my faith will produce the patience You desire in me. I give You all the glory and the honor.

Help me to continue to wait on You. Help me to seek You always. Lord. May You fill my cup to running over. I pray that my longings will be satisfied according to Your will. Fill me that I will rest from my wanderings.

Thank You, Lord, for Your love. Thank You for deliverance from my wilderness places. Your love never fails, it is everlasting. It does not hurt. Thank You for mending my heart. Thank You for forgiving me. Thank You for the Holy Spirit's directions. Thank You for listening. Thank You for hearing and answering my prayers. Your love is a comfort to all who will embrace You. As You embrace me, Lord, I rest all my cares upon Your chest and I bask in Your unchanging love.

Thank You for making me the apple of Your eyes. Thank You for reminding me that there is a comforter within. Thank You for Your grace and Your mercy. Thank You for healing my heart. Thank You for the miracle of restored health. Thank You for covering me. Thank You for being my loving Father and the Lover of my soul. Thank You for never leaving me. Thank You for peace. Now that I am growing in You, I thank You for my Joy. I bless Your name, my Father. If I have failed in asking anything of You, fail not to grant. For it is in Jesus's name that I petition your throne.

LOST LOVE

When Love let me down, it was so sudden

Why couldn't I see this would be the outcome?

Irony had replaced justice and despair had replaced love

The picture of Love is supposed to be perfect

Yet Love can hit so hard, one might not recognize its force

I have always personified Love as light as a feather,

Soft to the touch, unraveling you with its mysteries

When least expected, swish! Off your feet

Good thoughts swirling around your hollow

Love is sweet yet indescribable

What is it? Could it be manna?

Who can truly describe the taste?

But Love seems to have the ability to do harm to the mind, infecting the flesh and sending even the sanest mind into a tailspin

Somebody, stop this thing they call love; it does too much damage

Once you grab hold of the baton, its magnet infects the soul

If only you knew

There is a law of Love

It is potent, dangerous, and hazardous to one's health

Yet we pursue after it at breakneck speed

It is no wonder no one can stop it

Love is there, then it's not

It caresses, then it disappoints

Is it love that does this, or is it our minds that transform love into what it is not?

Today, I lost love because I loved too much

Today, I let love go because I still want to love

I have vowed not to seek after love again; love does not want to be pursued

Its primary power is to seek me and find me

So, my lost loves,

I will always love you, even though you don't know I love you

Esther C. Nurse

LOVE AT FIRST SIGHT

I am sure every time the heart is captivated, it sways
to a tune only ears could comprehend

It's spellbinding how the eyes see, yet the message
returned is seldom what the heart feels

Sometimes I feel this heart doesn't understand its function

Doesn't he see me? Can't he hear the rushing of two hearts?

Surely it must hear its own sound

Emotions are so magnetic, that's how one knows the heart hears

Yet he didn't even notice me

I wore my best, borrowed nonetheless

My heart wanted him to notice, drumming its loudest tunes

There he is, I gasp, from the mesmerizing tune my heart plays

So close to him, two hearts escalating with passion

Make that one heart that beats to the rhythm
no one else understands, not even him

How could he not hear my heart?

Images are formed in imaginations; to personify
the heart is the extent of sight and sound

There are those who say the mind is in the heart and the heart
overflows with information that allows the lips to speak…

Now I understand

He didn't notice me nor did he speak to me because his
heart is too blind and too deaf to hear a sound

She felt the beating of two hearts because she did not understand
that his heart was blind and there was no love at first sight

Perhaps she will never find love

For her heart is in a constant overflow

She lives in a world where sight is a handicap
and blindness is the norm

Love at first sight! I say, Nay

I wish they would cover their eyes because the
heart is blind and hears no sound

There is no such thing as love at first sight!

He didn't even notice me.

Esther C. Nurse

Afterword

In my quest to find healing for my body and my heart, I was reintroduced to a special scripture. I pray that someone will find deliverance in this scripture while passing through or coming out of a storm. My storm right now is my health. I want to be delivered from medication use; I want to be healthy. I want to live.

The scripture is found in James 1:2-8:

My brethren, Count it all joy when you fall into various trials, knowing that the testing of your faith produces patience. But let patience have its perfect work, that you may be perfect and complete, lacking nothing. ***If any of you lacks wisdom, let him ask of God, who gives to all liberally and without reproach, and it will be given to him.*** *But let him ask in faith, with no doubting, for he who doubts is like a wave of the sea driven and tossed by the wind. For let not that man suppose that he will receive anything from the Lord; he is a double-minded man, unstable in all his way.* (NKJV)

There is much to glean from these few verses. God's voice has spoken to me. We are to ask for wisdom, we are to be patient, we are to be faithful, and we are to stand firm in our request of God. The binding line in this scripture is if anyone lacks wisdom in any decision making, from the most minute thing to the largest decision making, ask wisdom of God. In all of your plans, whether a relationship, marriage, childbearing, giving a response—and the list goes on—ask of God.

Another scripture says, "…yet you do not have because you do not ask" (James 4:2, NKJV). God wants His children to occupy until he returns; therefore, he has made provisions, leaving us promises, a compass to navigate the scriptures, and the Holy Spirit not only to comfort us but also to make intercession to God with our prayers.

Whether you have failed in love, become ill and disappointed, lost trust, feel lonely, mourn losses and broken marriages, want to purchase a house—you name it—God is a provider and a restorer. He will restore according to His will. As Jesus said, He came that we might have life, and have it abundantly. Give Him abundant praise for what He will do in your life today and every day until He returns.